PENGUIN BOOKS

THE PRACTICE OF NOT THINKING

Ryunosuke Koike was born in 1978 in Yamaguchi Prefecture, Japan.
A former Buddhist monk of the Jodo Shinshu School, he is now master
of the Tsukuyomi Hall, previously known as Tsukuyomi Temple, in
Kanagawa Prefecture. He is internationally renowned for his accessible,
yet comprehensive books on Zen and Buddhism, which have sold over
a million copies in Japan alone and have been translated into
many languages.

Eriko Sugita has translated several books including *Goodbye*, *Things* by
Fumio Sasaki. She was born in Japan, raised in Canada and has also
worked as a reporter and photojournalist.

RYUNOSUKE KOIKE

The Practice of Not Thinking

A Guide to Mindful Living

Translated by Eriko Sugita

PENGUIN BOOKS

PENGUIN BOOKS

UK | USA | Canada | Ireland | Australia
India | New Zealand | South Africa

Penguin Books is part of the Penguin Random House group of companies
whose addresses can be found at global.penguinrandomhouse.com

| Penguin
Random House
UK

This translation first published in Great Britain by Penguin Books 2021

017

This book is originally published in Japan by Shogakukan in February 2010.
Published as *Kangaenai Renshu* by Ryunosuke Koike.
Mass market paperback edition printed March 11, 2012

Set in 9.25/12.5 pt Sabon LT Std
Typeset by Integra Software Services Pvt. Ltd, Pondicherry

Printed and bound in Great Britain by Clays Ltd, Elcograf S.p.A.

The authorized representative in the EEA is Penguin Random House,
Morrison Chambers, 32 Nassau Street, Dublin D02 YH68

A CIP catalogue record for this book is available from the British Library

ISBN: 978-0-141-99461-1

www.greenpenguin.co.uk

MIX
Paper | Supporting
responsible forestry
FSC® C018179
www.fsc.org

Penguin Random House is committed to a
sustainable future for our business, our readers
and our planet. This book is made from Forest
Stewardship Council® certified paper.

Contents

CONTENTS

Introduction

All the failures that we ever experience may be attributed to excessive thinking, and in particular the negative thoughts that pop up in our mind.

We may start the day full of energy, telling ourselves that we're ready to take on the world. But somewhere along the way, the mind seems to take a direction of its own and tells us to slow down or to stop what we're doing as it's too much trouble. Or perhaps we were planning to take a ten-minute break and our mind decides to make it an hour.

These are just a couple of examples that show how our thoughts may not necessarily be governed by our own free will and how they can pull us into negative territory. Our thoughts can get in the way and prevent us from living the way we want. But looking at it from another angle, if we're able to control our mind, maybe we'll be able to stop the continuous thinking that goes on in our head, dictating how we behave.

The problem here is that the mind has a habit of looking for stronger stimulation and can get out of control if we let it. Because negative thoughts have a much stronger impact on our brain than a mild, gentle sense of happiness, it's hard to prevent that from happening.

In recent years, there has been a tendency to speak about the brain with a sense of awe and gratitude for its functions. But this information-processing device that we all have is a rogue entity that continues to forge ahead in search of thought-provoking stimuli, regardless of the effects on us and whether we'll end up suffering as a result.

The problem is that the brain continues to churn out thoughts, even when we want to stop thinking. For instance, it could very well be going on with incessant thoughts such as:

'Okay, I'm going to stop thinking right now.'

'Wait a minute, I didn't realize I was still thinking.'

'Oh dear, things just don't seem to go the way I want.'

'Come to think of it, the meal I cooked last night didn't turn out very well.'

'I'm starting to feel hungry.'

It's only after acknowledging that we can't stop these distracting noises – fragments of information that just end up exhausting us – from disturbing our peace of mind that we understand just how unaware we've been of the trains of thought that buzz through our mind on a regular basis. When we become aware that we haven't been noticing how these unstoppable thoughts continue to pop up in our mind, we begin to realize that we aren't really thinking in the way we thought we were or would like to be thinking.

Then maybe it's better not to think. But *thinking about not thinking* only means we're doing more thinking, and it isn't going to prevent us from thinking. We can try to convince ourselves that we've understood what's been happening, but the only way to gain control of our thinking is to practise stopping it.

The techniques that I outline in this book suggest ways to overcome our thinking, which can appear to have a will of its own. To do that, we can hone our five senses and bolster our perception of the physical. We'll focus on the five senses – sight, hearing, smell, taste and touch – and how we use them in our daily lives, and we'll practise controlling our thinking.

We tend to think too much because we can't control our thinking, and that can cause confusion in our thoughts and make our mind less sharp than it could be. Our goal is to stop thinking too much, prevent our thinking from getting tattered due to overuse, and to recharge our energy by practising the art of not thinking.

Once we've done that, our thoughts are sure to be crystal clear and full of inspiration.

I
A thinking disease

By thinking, we can become ignorant

WITHDRAWING INTO OUR BRAIN DECREASES OUR POWER OF CONCENTRATION

As humans, we are always thinking. Thinking is usually considered a fine characteristic of humanity, and we tend to believe we're superior to animals because we think. But is that truly the case?

My feeling is that because we think, our ability to concentrate can falter, and we can sometimes get frustrated or lost. Let's call it *thinking disease*, a disease that occurs as a result of thinking. And let us first take a moment to consider this.

It's often said that people today aren't very good at listening to what others have to say. Maybe it's because we've experienced being frustrated or angry when we wanted someone to listen to us and found that they hadn't taken in a word we said. Were they *that* uninterested?

They had made the time to talk to us, so they couldn't have been completely uninterested at the outset. They were probably willing to lend an ear to what we had to say, at least in the beginning. But what often happens is that once you begin to discuss your problem with someone, a host of irrelevant thoughts start to pop up in the other person's mind. Maybe they want to show you their willingness to listen so they can win your trust, or maybe they are pretending to be understanding so you will see them as a wonderful human being. It certainly

3

isn't the worst outcome you could expect since the person is there out of consideration for you. But they can't help it if other thoughts start to cross their mind, such as *'I'd love a beer right now'* or *'Which bar should I stop by after this?'*

As someone who practises Zen meditation, I watch the flow of my awareness over long periods of time. By doing that, I can see that my mind is working continually and at tremendous speed. It moves around incredibly quickly, processing information, and travels on to parts of my body that are related to the five senses, such as my eyes, through which it will watch, or it might go to my ears and start listening. And these actions take place in no more than split fragments of a second.

It's during these brief moments that information is processed. The mind may flit from listening to watching, then from listening to thinking, listening, watching and back to listening again, and so on. Although we may think that we're only listening to someone speak, what's passing through our mind is a colossal amount of information that includes a vast mass of things that are often completely irrelevant.

While someone who listens without paying particular attention to what another person is saying may think that all they're doing is listening, there are a myriad tiny snippets of information passing through their mind at the same time. These are the briefest moments in time in which we glimpse our favourite foods, drinks or flashes of strange images that we might encounter in a dream. They appear at speeds so fast that we don't even realize it, creating disruptions as we listen. A huge amount of noise from around us is thrown in and combined in minute moments, and our concentration starts – and continues – to break up.

I think it's fair to say that, among all our faculties, thinking is what requires the greatest amount of effort. We use words to think, thus locking ourselves within the act of thinking and forgetting about our other faculties. It therefore makes sense that the more our thoughts take charge of our brain, the less information we're able to absorb from what is going on around us. We sometimes aren't aware of what is going on and what it means because we're unconsciously allocating a lot of energy to the process of thinking.

4

We don't think about so many things when we're relaxed. The number of thoughts we have and the time we spend on them increase when we're confused. Let's say you're watching a movie and there's something in the back of your mind that continues to bother you. It will prompt more noise to seep into your mind as you sit there trying to watch the film.

When we're walking hand in hand with a loved one, especially a partner in a long-term relationship, there's always a physical sense of touch that registers in our mind and makes us aware that we're holding hands. But if we're contemplating something else at that moment, the act of holding hands won't seem real, and we probably won't get into the right mood to enjoy it. One of us might be thinking about work while the other could be thinking about some other person. The two of us are together and there's physical contact between us, but neither is in the same place mentally. It's because we've both locked ourselves inside our brains.

THE THREE DISTURBING EMOTIONS: DESIRE, ANGER AND UNCERTAINTY

It's natural to get caught up in our thoughts and not be fully present when we are with our partner. It happens to a lot of people. Think back to when you first met your beloved. Everything about your budding relationship must have been fresh and exciting at the time. More specifically, you were seeing fresh, new images of that appealing person, and your heart began fluttering in response to the new stimulation. You were tuned in to that person, noticed the smallest changes in their hairstyle, wondered if they were bored if their face happened to cloud over even slightly, and you would quickly come up with something interesting to talk about.

But our mind gradually gets used to receiving information about that person. In reality, the face is just one part of a person in which changes continue to occur at lightning speed, but we become less attentive, to the extent it no longer appears that they're changing at all. This is what generally happens when we become bored with someone.

We continue to pick up the same types of information about them, but it's no longer novel, it isn't exciting, and we start to look for other things that stimulate us.

Some people then go looking for someone else. Others, meanwhile, retreat to the ideal lover in their mind, though it doesn't necessarily have to be a man or a woman – it can be something that we like to do. Then we start to get absorbed in that 'lover' – whether or not it's personified – and as all of this happens in our mind, we escape inside ourselves and begin to lose interest in the person who had once been the focus of our attention.

Some people get bored quickly, while it's more gradual for others. This boredom is deeply connected with what in Buddhism we call kleshas (literally 'poisons') or disturbing emotions. Allow me to take a moment to briefly explain what these are.

We're constantly receiving different types of information through our eyes, ears, nose, tongue, body (sense of touch) and our awareness. There are various impulsive energies of the mind that respond to such stimuli, the significant ones being 'the three poisons': desire, anger and uncertainty.

Desire refers to the impulsive energy in our mind that continues to want more and more when we see or hear things. For example, say someone compliments us. Regardless of how empty such compliments may be, our klesha energy for desire is fully activated, we soar sky-high and become hungry for more praise.

Then there's anger, which I define as impulsive energy of the mind that is resistant to the information provided by the senses and rejects it. When someone makes a nasty remark and we become uncomfortable, our klesha energy for anger is roused, and it tries to push away and eliminate whatever it is that's unpleasant.

Anger is much broader in its implications in our daily lives than you might think. It includes everything from the negative energy that prevents us from feeling motivated, makes us jealous of others or causes us to regret the past, to feeling lonely or getting nervous. Anger is at the root of these intrusive thoughts, and it feeds on our negative energy.

Vague ideas of bad things briefly surface and then disappear in a flash. Because of this, we often experience a sense of unease without knowing the reason for it. Such unconscious thoughts pop in and out of our mind so quickly that we aren't even aware of what's happening, and they become the trigger for chain reactions of thoughts that propel us down a negative track by *making us* think.

For example, we might start out being shocked by something that has happened, move on to concerns about what might happen if we fail at whatever it is that we're doing, and start worrying about certain people making fun of us should that happen. In other words, our *thinking* starts to get out of control.

The more these monologues in our mind increase in volume, the more our memory will be invaded by meaningless thoughts, which can lead to a diminishing sense of satisfaction. We might stop being able to take in properly the sights and sounds of the world around us, the expressions on the faces of the people in front of us and the sounds of their voices; we might stop appreciating our favourite foods, even when we're eating them, because we can no longer focus.

We may think we're seeing, hearing or touching something, but because our memory is preoccupied by thoughts of the past that keep buzzing in our head, there's no room for new information to be taken in. We may listen to someone speak to us for one second and hear what they're saying for 0.1 seconds, but the remaining 0.9 seconds are vague because of the dominant thinking and noise from the past that keep interrupting, making us wonder how the person feels about us. It numbs our senses and makes things hard to absorb.

Keep this up and we'll lose out on nine out of ten seconds and a genuine appreciation of reality for fifty-four out of sixty minutes. And by the time we grow old, we'll be looking back and marvelling at how quickly those years have flown by. As a consequence of losing ourselves in our thoughts, which are sometimes fantasies that do not tie in with what's actually happening, our sense of reality will be depleted, as will our feeling of happiness.

Many people start to talk about how quickly time seems to be going by as they get older. This is because the noise created by the thoughts that they have carefully preserved in their mind over time accumulates and blocks any new information that tries to enter.

And I feel that it's often when that noise achieves a complete victory over the sense of reality that people might start to become senile in old age. Because they become solely controlled by information from the past and unable to accept new realities, they may even see a grandchild, recognize him as their son, and be unable to correct that misconception.

The root cause for all of that can be narrowed down to the idea that the reality in front of us is too ordinary, too boring, and that negative thoughts are stimulating. In our mind's search for new stimuli, our thoughts are programmed to go out of control in seeking the negative. We easily fall victim to this *thinking disease* without realizing it, and before we know it, we gradually become impervious, our mind closed to new influences, and more prone to becoming senile in old age. Once we understand that, it should help to silence the pointless chatter in our mind.

It's the impulsive energy of the mind that I mentioned earlier that causes us to become bored with what is in front of us. It impels us to start looking for new stimuli, which is what makes us *lose direction*. Someone may be talking to us, but our mind drifts as if to highlight that the conversation is boring and that we should ignore that person. We zone out from the conversation and end up taking in nothing from the speaker. This is a klesha, or disturbing emotion, of being lost or confused, known as the klesha of ignorance or uncertainty.

In this case, the word ignorance does not imply that a person is uncultured or lacks intelligence. It means they're unaware of the types of thoughts that are going through their head and the ways in which their conscious mind is working at that particular moment.

When we think, our energy is spent on the act of thinking. It means our other senses – sight, hearing, smell, taste and touch – tend to become dulled. Because we're so focused on thinking about various things, our physical senses are neglected, and our mind and body become out of sync.

The more we overwork a particular part of our brain, the less we're able to perceive physical information, and the more 'ignorant' or confused we become. We're unable to gain a firm grasp of the changes that occur in another person's voice or facial expressions, and they'll always seem to be the same – boring – according to our perception of them.

The more thinking that we do in our mind alone, the more useless thoughts we'll accumulate. And when that happens, we become impervious to reality and the flow of our own thoughts. The klesha of ignorance will make us seek an escape from reality to the safety of the thoughts in our mind. Once we make it a habit, we easily develop a tendency to withdraw into our own thoughts, and it is hard to break out of that.

TRAINING TO DISCIPLINE THE MIND IN THE RIGHT WAY

Up to this point, I have said that people become ignorant because they think. But of course it doesn't mean that we shouldn't think.

In Buddhism, there is something known as the Noble Eightfold Path that people are encouraged to strive to follow in order to live the right way. The eight elements can be categorized within three main steps:

Step 1 – Setting rules for yourself and developing an inner strength that will prevent you from faltering
>   The right thoughts (to correct your thoughts)
>   The right speech (to correct your speech)
>   The right conduct (to correct your actions)
>   The right livelihood (to correct the way you live)

Step 2 – Developing your concentration
>   The right concentration
>   The right cleansing of the mind

Step 3 – Becoming aware
>   The right mindfulness (to hone the sensors of your mind)
>   The right views (to enable you to understand)

The first part of the first step is to have the right thoughts, as indicated at the top of the list, or to think in the correct way. It means considering the bare essentials. For example, it means thinking about the best order for washing the dishes when you're standing in front of the kitchen sink after dinner, how to use the smallest amount of water necessary and how to use as little dishwashing liquid as possible.

If your mind is clogged with unneeded kleshas – disturbing emotions – you'll look at the leftover food on the plate your child had been using and feel irritated, wondering why he never eats all his food. But that irritation is doubly pointless. For a start, you'll get careless about washing the dishes properly and efficiently if you're feeling frustrated. And getting annoyed with your child isn't an effective way to make him finish his dinner. Instead of getting irritated, you should stay calm and collected. You could say something like this:

'I make the meals for everyone in our family, and I feel very sad when you don't eat everything I put on the table. I feel unhappy throwing away the leftovers when I do the dishes. I don't want to be unhappy like this, and I'm sure you aren't happy to see me unhappy, either. So, why don't you try to make an effort to eat everything on your plate?'

Similarly, if you're spending time with your beloved, the best thing to do is to think about what the two of you can do in the moment to enjoy being together instead of recalling trouble you may have had at work earlier in the day.

Not thinking in a way that tires you, thinking only the most appropriate thoughts in a particular moment, eliminating unrestrained thoughts and ideas that go around and around in your mind, and overcoming your kleshas. These are the challenges we face as we begin our journey in Buddhism, and they're also the goals that we aim to achieve.

KEEPING YOUR SENSES ACTIVE HELPS MAINTAIN A BALANCED STATE OF MIND

Meditation is the most effective training for achieving those goals. But what if you don't have the opportunity to meditate?

You can't overcome those excess thoughts that resound in your mind if you aren't even aware that your thoughts have drifted or you're thinking useless thoughts. The first thing to do is to pay attention to the movements of your mind on a regular basis. Check yourself now and then, setting up an imaginary sensor in the same way that you would set up an alarm system for your home, and ask yourself these questions:

'*What is my mind thinking about now?*'
'*What is it looking at?*'
'*What is it listening to?*'
'*What types of smells is it smelling?*'

If you do this regularly, the moment will eventually come when realization dawns. You'll be spending time with someone, intending to enjoy their company, when you become aware that your mind is drifting off, dwelling on things that are completely irrelevant. You'll be conscious that your mind has started to get obsessed with idle thoughts.

Once you become aware that this is happening, the next step is to adjust your awareness or change the movements of your mind. If you find that you're *thinking* unneeded thoughts, you should focus on *feeling* instead. Let's say you're touching or kissing someone. You can transfer your awareness to the sense of touching with your lips. Make a conscious effort to deepen that awareness and those other thoughts will quietly start to diminish.

You don't have to be able to create a special state of awareness to control your mind to a certain extent. In Buddhism, the ability to become aware is called the *power of the will*. The will refers to our ability to recognize things, like a sensor for awareness. The more fine-tuned that sensor is, the more sensitive we are to the smallest changes.

Once we become aware of that, another capacity that we have is the power to concentrate so we can change how our mind works. We concentrate, control our awareness, grab hold of it and focus on it in a single location. It means gathering up and bringing together in one place the scattered thoughts that flit through our mind at lightning speed.

The first thing is to make it a habit to recognize how many of your five senses you're using at any particular time.

SATISFYING YOUR MIND BY
RESPONDING TO YOUR SENSES

I've just mentioned the five senses. Buddhist belief has it that, in addition to the eyes, ears, nose, tongue and body (sense of touch), there is a sixth 'sense door' of awareness that recognizes external stimulation. When information is received through these six doors, we become aware that we are seeing, hearing, smelling, tasting, touching or thinking. You can refer to these six doors in the quick-reference checklist at the end of this book. And it's through this sixth door that we become aware of *our inner self* – our identity – that we recognize as the person that we are.

To become aware of which of our five senses we're using at any time, we need to be actively conscious of them and not going about aimlessly in our daily lives. Note the differences between the following:

The passive state of seeing and the active state of looking.

The passive state of hearing and the active state of listening.

The passive state of noticing a smell and the active state of smelling something.

The passive state of tasting something and the active state of savouring it.

The passive state of touching something and the active state of feeling it.

Try the following simple exercises:

At this moment, you are probably 'seeing' an overview of the scene in front of you. Now, direct your attention to a particular object. Something small is best. Look at it, focus on it and don't look away. Stop your awareness from straying to anything else around you and focus on 'seeing' that one item alone.

That's the difference between 'seeing' and 'looking'. By actively looking at that one object, the other things around it will fade into the background and your other senses will gradually calm down. That isn't to say that you'll be unable to hear any of the sounds around you.

You'll be focusing on looking while vaguely hearing and experiencing other physical sensations at the same time.

Something else you can do is to focus your attention on the surface of your skin that's now exposed, such as one of your hands or your face. Try to feel the physical sensation of the air touching it. Maybe it's raining outside, and the air feels a little cold and damp. Stop thinking about the temperature and surrender yourself to the sensation, the stimulation on your skin. Try to focus on that sensation and you will find that it can be quite comfortable and you will feel at peace regardless of the temperature.

Next, let's try to concentrate on the feeling of your body enclosed beneath the clothing you're wearing. This time, you should feel a change in the temperature from the previous exercise. It will be a pleasant sensation that comes not from a sense of physical pleasure but rather from the comfort of a focused mental state where you've stopped processing information and remain within the feeling you've achieved.

That's the difference between *touching* and actually *feeling*. In a Buddhist context, it's the difference between *forgetting* and *focusing*.

As you practise being active with your senses in these ways, you will stop being affected by the various noises incurred by your thoughts, becoming clearly aware of the information in front of you at any given moment, and your mind will start to achieve a sense of fulfilment.

You will enable yourself to focus your awareness – which had been distracted by thoughts that occur as you look vaguely at something, think about something irrelevant, listen to various sounds or feel the cold weather – on specific things that you truly need to do.

Since ancient times, Japanese people have had the ability to regard the sounds in nature, such as raindrops or water running or falling, as interesting subjects, and they have enjoyed capturing in art or literature the elegance of the natural world around them. But because new sources of stimulation are created and sought in modern times, they are losing such refined and delicate sensibilities.

Shift your mindset from *hearing* to *listening*, *seeing passively* to *seeing intentionally*, practise sharpening your five senses, and you will begin to feel a sense of fulfilment from contemplating things that may appear at first to be boring. Maybe you sometimes feel that your days aren't all that exciting. By practising this drill, you'll enable yourself to achieve a more delicate and refined sense of awareness of the world around you and start to enjoy it without the need to resort to more overtly stimulating types of entertainment that simply fill your brain with a lot of noise.

By sharpening your awareness sensor that interprets the data obtained by your five senses, while taking a fresh look at your life in general, you will eventually notice that frustration and uncertainty have faded from your mind and your temperament may even have improved in the process. You'll be able to focus on your work, studies or whatever task you have in hand at that moment, your attention no longer straying to what is around you or what you might prefer to be doing.

In the next chapter, we will consider specific ways to cure *thinking disease* by taking a look at our everyday actions and communication methods, such as seeing, speaking, listening or behaving attentively. Besides achieving a balance between your mind and your body, once you figure out the programming that your mind has been controlled by, you'll start to let go and shrug off the heavy load of accumulated noise that has been weighing you down.

II
How to control your body and your mind

Steps to eliminate frustration and uncertainty

I. SPEAKING

You may think that the words we speak are guided by our own free will. However, as I mentioned in the previous chapter, using correct speech is part of the Noble Eightfold Path, and it is very difficult to do.

Let's say that you're meeting an important business associate. Seeing this person will have an immediate impact on you and how you feel you should behave, and once you start thinking along those lines, it'll be hard to stop yourself. In less than one-thousandth of a second, you'll almost certainly be overwhelmed by an urge to say something nice to that person to create a good impression. Maybe you'll start talking about the weather:

'Unfortunately, the rain's been going on for a while.'

'Oh, but what a smart umbrella you have. What brand is it?'

You don't particularly dislike the rain, but you go with the social convention that it's something unpleasant and say things that reflect this. You aren't interested in the designs of umbrellas, and you aren't interested in specific brands, but you pretend to be interested so that you can compliment the person. At that moment, maybe you'll wonder why you made that comment and say to yourself, 'That isn't what I'm really thinking.' You'll be aware of these tiny lies that you've told without realizing it, and little by little, those niggling thoughts will plant themselves within your subconscious and build stress. That happens because your mind automatically responds to the visual impact made on it by the person in question, and you start to think without realizing it.

Here's another example. You're bragging to someone about something you've done; the person smiles and tells you how much you have impressed them and what a fantastic individual you must be. Their voice registers in your mind, stimulates your sense of desire, and you end up speaking more quickly and loudly about your accomplishments.

Although we may believe that we're thinking and speaking of our own free will, what's happening is (a) our mind is inputting information triggered by a particular form of stimulation, and (b) it is automatically reacting and providing output. Blunders occur when we don't know how to control this reaction. We say words reflexively because we don't know how to respond to the stimuli that have entered our mind. We aren't *speaking* as much as *being made to speak* by the stimulant, and we will continue regretting our words as long as this process continues.

Let's think about specific ways to free our mind from being locked into such a state, so that we can speak with more freedom and elegance.

OBSERVE THE TONE OF YOUR VOICE AS A BASIS FOR SPEECH

Let us consider the first essential step of vocalization. We're likely to be tempted to include as much information as we can in our speech when we want someone to listen to us. The stronger the klesha of desire to gain the person's attention, the more we'll tend to speak in a loud, rapid-fire voice.

The irony is that, although we're speaking loudly and rapidly because we want the person to listen to us, the impact that we make on them will be unpleasant. As a result, we'll provoke their klesha of anger, whether we're trying to convince them of something or attempting to brag, making it tougher to obtain their agreement.

On the other hand, people will be able to relax and listen to us if we speak at a relaxed speed and a moderate pitch. It's a good idea to begin by being considerate, thinking of our listener, so we don't cause unnecessary stimulation or stress for the other person. To do that, I would like to suggest always lending an ear to your voice. Focus on the effect created by the sounds that echo in your throat.

Everyone tends to believe they know how they sound when they speak. The truth of the matter is that we don't have complete control over our voice. When we're speaking with someone, we continue to *think* about what the other person is saying, what we want to say and how the other person will feel about what we say to them. In other words, our voice is something that we hear only incidentally during the conversations that we have.

Try to move away from that and make a conscious effort to focus on your voice, and you'll realize that how it sounds is quite different from what you may have thought. But be careful not to push yourself. You don't want to force yourself *to think* that you have to speak more slowly or gently. Simply be aware of the act of concentrating on your voice. As long as you maintain that awareness, it will be natural for your mind to notice that something isn't right when you start to speak too rapidly or when the pitch of your voice becomes too high. In the same way that we feel uncomfortable when someone babbles in a voice that's too loud, our mind will automatically register any changes, as long as we keep looking at ourselves objectively.

It isn't unusual for people to hear their voice on an answering machine and be surprised at how rapidly they speak or how high-pitched their voice is. But by making it a habit to observe themselves objectively, they will notice when they start to talk too quickly or too loudly and thus end up inflicting a lot of distracting stimulation upon the people around them. That awareness will eventually rid them of such habits and help them speak more moderately.

It's also useful to stop and wait for a moment if you realize that you're speaking too rapidly. It'll calm your nerves and also allow the person who's listening to take a break. People tend to stop wanting things when those items are available in excess, and they seek them when they have rarity value, so it might be useful to offer a little less than what you consider to be enough. It should appeal to those on the receiving end.

As Buddha says in scripture, we should try to speak clearly and in a moderate tone – not too fast, not too slow, and in a voice that is neither too high- nor too low-pitched.

ARROGANCE PROMPTS YOU TO TALK BACK TO PEOPLE

I think that, at some point in their lives, everyone will have talked back to someone when it hasn't been necessary. What happens is that when we receive negative stimuli due to something that someone has said to us, our mind issues a command to go ahead and make a retort. Let's say your boss approaches you with a remark like this:

'*I think it's about time you got working on that assignment.*'

The moment the words have registered with your sense of hearing, your klesha of arrogance gets switched on. Then your thoughts start to go wild.

Arrogance is one of the kleshas of the desire to cling to your pride, where you worry about how other people see and evaluate you. While we want people to look at us in a positive light, what's stronger is our desire to maintain our image and sense of self-worth.

'*My boss is worried that I'm not going to do that assignment. He's convinced that I won't get started if he doesn't push me.*'

'*It wasn't as if I'd forgotten about it. I was planning to get to it.*'

'*I'm not as useless as my boss thinks I am.*'

'*That boss is an idiot who simply doesn't appreciate me.*'

As soon as you hear your boss's remark, various thoughts start running riot in your mind, and an uncalled-for retort is your reflexive response. Or maybe you'll be more positive and say something like:

'*Oh, sorry. I thought it would be better to do this after seeing the results in our meeting next week. But I'll do it now if you insist.*'

You're apologizing, but there's a negative note in what you're saying as you suggest that it'll be your boss's fault for making you do the assignment now and producing mediocre results.

When you think about it logically, the best thing to do would be to proceed with the assignment at once without talking back to your boss. If you honestly believe that it would be more rational to start working on it after your meeting, then you can carefully explain that to your boss, and he should understand. But because you're being motivated by the klesha of arrogance, in which you don't want to feel rejected and want your boss to think well of you, you end up making a half-hearted effort to apologize and you talk back without getting on straight away with the assignment.

PRACTISE ELIMINATING YOUR NEGATIVE THOUGHTS

What, then, should we do when we're irritated or feel an urge to talk back to someone?

We can broadly split into two the responses that we generally make when we feel a negative emotion. The first is to work off our anger or frustration, such as by complaining. The second is to repress our emotions, controlling the feelings that we experience, turning our back on what took place and forcing ourselves to pretend that nothing happened.

With the former, our anger becomes further etched on our mind as we complain. That energy builds and builds until it's on fire, giving us a lot of stimulation, and our mind often confuses that with a good feeling. As we continue along that path, we gradually become short-tempered. A precondition is created for our brain to remember that taking out our anger on someone else stimulates our mind and makes us feels good, which in turn prompts us to become touchy and quick to let our anger surface.

But despite attempting to control that agitation, we end up igniting another type of anger. It's an emotion which tells us that it's not right to be furious on impulse. We thus generate complicated feelings within us, and as our anger-on-anger battles continue, our personality will gradually become distorted.

What I recommend from a Buddhist perspective is to avoid both these responses. Instead of releasing your anger or holding it back, you can *observe* your own emotions.

If you feel irritated by someone, **immediately set those emotions aside**. You firmly believe that those feelings are genuine. There's no question in your mind that they must be the ultimate truth. Now put those feelings in brackets and repeat to yourself:

(I'm irritated – I think.)

(I'm irritated – I think.)

By doing that, realize that you only *think* that you're irritated, and it isn't the absolute truth. Be aware that it's only an emotion in your mind. The words that go in the brackets can be any variation of the above:

(I thought I was irritated.)

(The person in front of me is irritated.)

(My boss might be irritated, but so am I.)

The important thing is to be aware that this sense of irritation is a single perspective – it's only one viewpoint. By taking a step back and examining your frustration from a broader standpoint, you'll learn to accept it. By isolating and acknowledging the existence of the emotion from a third-party perspective, neither affirming nor denying it, you will stop yourself from responding reflexively.

You can objectively observe your mind by repeating to yourself a few times using the same words that you only *think* you're irritated. Setting your thoughts within brackets like this, you'll be able to contain your thinking and prevent it from getting out of control. That way, you'll be able to see things clearly.

By taking a moment to pause in this way, you'll be able to develop a more considered, logical response as to whether you will do as your boss says or come up with an alternative plan of action.

WHEN APOLOGIZING, OFFER SPECIFIC SUGGESTIONS FOR IMPROVEMENT

When you think about it, the world is full of apologies and excuses:

'I'm sorry I couldn't contact you sooner.'

'Excuse me for repeatedly calling you.'

But if people started responding honestly to such words, saying,

'*You'd better be sorry!*' or '*I'm swamped!*' the person apologizing would undoubtedly be taken aback.

We all know that, following social convention, these types of apologies are always accepted with a '*No problem*' or '*Don't worry about it*'. It's when someone doesn't accept our apology and forgive us that we may become irritated or perhaps even angry, amazed at how narrow-minded and unforgiving that person is. And what becomes clear once we've become angry is that we weren't serious about offering an apology in the first place.

Then why is it that we apologize? Why do we make excuses? It's because we don't want the other person to think we're rude. That's the thought that instantly fills our mind. And more than that: we don't want to believe that we're rude.

If we're truly sorry about something, we should think about the best way to ease the burden on the other person rather than merely apologizing or making an excuse for our own comfort. Otherwise, it can become a habit to offer simple apologies and make excuses, and it will then become tough to convey our sincere regret when we're genuinely sorry. Think about that, control the thoughts that make you apologize and gradually cut back on those instant apologies.

Still, there are times when it's necessary from a social standpoint to apologize, even if you aren't truly sorry. There's been a delay in your delivering work by the promised deadline or you've made a mistake and someone is angry. There are various situations in which an apology is needed. To calmly take stock of the situation and determine the type of apology required, you need to *think*.

The person affected by your blunder will be able to see through an insincere apology that doesn't come from the heart, and you won't be able to convey your regret.

When an apology is needed, rather than merely saying you're sorry, it's best to say you'll be careful not to make the same mistake again. The right tone of voice and a humble expression on your face, together with an account of the specific steps you plan to take to make things better, should accompany a genuine apology.

With that in mind, you'll succeed in communicating your earnest desire to improve. You'll be indicating specific steps for resolving the issue at hand, which will prevent the other person from becoming annoyed and make it easier for him or her to forgive you.

'*Okay, please do that.*'

That's the likely response that you will receive. The other person may even want to assist in devising ways for you to improve.

But please note that you will need to follow through on your suggestions in order to gain that person's trust. Although people generally forgive you for making a mistake the first time, repeating it two or three times gives them the impression that you aren't serious. Rather than thinking that you've apologized, all is well and the issue is over, view it as an opportunity for your personal development and stick to your word.

SELF-SERVING EXCUSES WILL ONLY INFLICT MORE PAIN ON THE OTHER PERSON

But when you think about it, it may be tough to stop making excuses. Let's say you've put your culinary skills to work and prepared a meal for your family, friends or significant other. You've served everyone and sampled the food yourself, and it occurs to you that the flavour may have been too bland. The stimulation from that tasting overwhelms you. Your mind gets busy in a whirlwind of thoughts. Then, you reflexively set out to make a horde of excuses, along the lines of:

'*Oh, I'm sorry, I forgot to check the food before serving it. Was it a little bland? I'm so sorry – things have been a bit hectic today.*'

Although you probably wanted to say something quite different:

'*I'm actually a pretty good cook – as long as I have the chance to taste what I make in advance. There wouldn't have been a problem if I'd had ample time to prepare this meal.*'

To the people around you, it will seem as though you're just talking to yourself. It's not so bad if that's the extent of your excuses, but once you start giving explanations, it'll become a habit. You will begin pointlessly repeating yourself. Every time someone eats what you make, you will end up asking them if it tastes okay, that you happened to make a mistake with the seasonings, and so on. You will in effect be pressurizing the person to give you a positive response, and they'll tell you that it's okay, the food tastes good, and the effort is likely to exhaust them. Not only are *you* thinking, but you'll also be making the other person think.

You won't be torturing them if they like the taste of the food. But if not, they will be accumulating stress by being forced to lie to themselves and tell you that it's lovely. You will be stressing them out with the pressure to follow up with positive comments after you've made excuses, and the act of making excuses doesn't make you feel all that comfortable, either. Why, then, is it that you continue to do this?

It becomes a habit. Your mind becomes addicted to the stimulation of resulting pain. It deludes you into believing that the sense of anxiety that you get from painful stimulation feels good, and it rewrites what should be uncomfortable as something that gives you pleasure. The temporary sense of feeling helpful fools you, you give your mind free rein and the cycle is repeated again and again. You're fooled by the trap to rewrite the information you receive, that your food is excellent, convincing yourself instead that no one is likely to believe that you're a good cook who just happened to have been too busy to do better on that particular day.

Let's see through these klesha mechanisms, avoid being caught in the trap of rewriting information and gain the self-control to stop firing away with harmful excuses.

A SINCERE APOLOGY FROM THE HEART WILL EASE THE OTHER PERSON'S PAIN

I'm not saying that all excuses are harmful, as there are times when a reason or explanation can ease the other person's mental burden.

You don't have to apologize as though it's the end of the world if you're five minutes late for a meeting. It should be enough to say you're sorry to be late with a frank but sincere expression on your face. But if you're so late that you know you will have annoyed the other person, it's your responsibility to ease that annoyance. You're the one who has imprinted in that person's mind that they were made to wait, which has triggered negative stimulation, causing them to suffer. Their arrogance klesha has been activated. Maybe they're thinking:

'Do I mean so little to this person that they can't be bothered to get here on time to see me? Do they think it's okay to make me wait because I mean nothing to them?'

The way to treat that wound is to tell them that they have nothing to do with the fact that you are late. You should offer a sincere apology and explain that unavoidable circumstances caused the delay. Of course, that doesn't mean you can lie and say the train service had stopped when it hadn't. A lie like that would only serve to distort your own thinking processes.

The truth of the matter is that an excuse is neither always necessary nor unnecessary. A sincere apology or explanation may be useful if (a) the other person is suffering negative emotions due to your words or actions, and (b) they will be comforted if you give them a sincere apology or explanation. An excuse isn't something that you should fire off without a second thought. Before you do, you should assess the situation carefully while considering the other person's personality and the emotions that may have been provoked.

SHORT- AND LONG-TERM INTERESTS MISCONSTRUED BY THE BRAIN

There are occasions when we can't get to a particular place on time for an appointment, no matter how hard we try. It isn't uncommon in this situation to call ahead and say we'll get there in less time than it will take. We know it'll take another fifteen minutes, but why is it that we indicate our arrival will be in five minutes instead – and later regret it?

There's no question that the person waiting for us would rather hear the truth – that they will have to wait for another fifteen minutes. It would probably be more annoying if you said you would be there in five minutes and failed to show up for an extra ten minutes after that.

It's annoying both for the person who's doing the waiting and for you as the one who's making them wait. Making someone wait is significantly stressful on a subconscious level because the noise that enters your mind reaches fever pitch as you start wondering what they'll think of you. You want to respond to the other person's hopes that you'll soon be with them. You don't want to let them down, and you find yourself in a state of panic. The klesha of arrogance takes over, which only makes matters worse.

The consequences of being over-optimistic about one's time of arrival may not be too serious, but it can be a different story in the workplace when we give our word that we can get something done without considering whether it can be done or that it may not be doable. That can be risky, as a failure to deliver will damage your reputation, making people see you as a person who is all talk and unreliable, so that they no longer trust you with significant projects.

It can also happen when you're talking with your friends. Everyone's on a roll, you don't want to spoil the mood and you agree to do something you don't want to do. Here, too, you'll lose your friends' trust if you repeatedly fail to produce results.

Why do we make empty promises of this kind? It's because our mind automatically assesses the situation or the atmosphere, and our *thoughts* then jump the gun at lightning speed. Next comes the klesha of arrogance, in which we don't want others to think negatively of us or see us as incompetent.

It's the klesha of arrogance that stops us from acknowledging our inability to do something. It's a sign that our disturbing emotions are reflexively jumping to the forefront of our mind and getting in the way. We know that, in the long term, failure to deliver will damage our reputation and destroy people's trust in us, yet it's easy to plump instead for quick results.

Maybe the human brain is made in such a way that we tend to focus on short-term interests and overlook the long-term benefits. These things happen so often that I sometimes wonder if we focus only on the amount of stimulation we can achieve from moment to moment rather than looking further ahead. To prove that, we tend not to appreciate the long-term consequences of our actions, when we may lose someone's trust in us, and instead seek refuge in the stimulation of needlessly blaming ourselves.

SPEAKING ILL OF OTHERS WILL
EVENTUALLY DARKEN YOUR HEART

It is the starting point and goal of Buddhism to maintain control over the mind. We seek to endure disturbing emotions such as the kleshas of desire, anger and uncertainty by establishing and adhering to rules of self-discipline. It is through those rules that we control the energy of our kleshas.

Japanese Buddhism has ten precepts, which are called *juzenkai*. They are as follows:

1. Abstention from killing (to abstain from killing living beings).
2. Abstention from theft (to abstain from stealing something that you have not been given).
3. Abstention from sexual misconduct (to abstain from cheating on your loved one).
4. Abstention from false speech (to abstain from speaking of things that aren't true).
5. Abstention from vulgar language (to abstain from criticizing others).
6. Abstention from negative language (to abstain from spreading negative rumours).
7. Abstention from engaging in idle chatter (to abstain from forcing others to listen to idle chit-chat).
8. Abstention from greed (to abstain from creating room in the mind for greed).
9. Abstention from generating anger (to abstain from creating room in the mind for wrath).
10. Abstention from following wrong views (to adhere instead to the principles of impermanence, suffering and non-self).

You will notice that four out of the ten precepts have to do with speaking. It is best to avoid using vulgar language and bad-mouthing others, regardless of whether the person on the receiving end is not present and hence might not be hurt. Anger will poison the speaker's mind and increase that klesha. Because such words provide powerful stimulation, they will be fed right back as soon as the speaker says them and will deeply penetrate and pollute his or her mind.

Although we may delude ourselves into thinking that, by criticizing or speaking ill of someone, we can hold on to a sense of superiority that we're better than them, the only thing that's happening is that we're increasing the klesha of anger in our mind.

The same applies to abstention from negative language. People who gossip over harmful rumours about someone who isn't present will amplify the klesha of anger related to harming others. They will only be feeding back the negative energy to their own mind.

DOES CONTINUOUS LYING MAKE US LESS INTELLIGENT?

Abstention from false speech means not telling lies. Start talking about information that isn't true, and you'll be overwriting the correct information in your mind with incorrect data. False details will become embedded in your mind, which will affect its capacity to process information and mess up the links within your memory over the long term.

Say you lie about a pretty necklace you bought yourself and tell a friend that your boyfriend bought it for you. The links in your memory will be jumbled when you overwrite the correct information with 'He *bought it and gave it to me as a present*'.

The energy that messes up the links in your memory is the klesha of uncertainty or ignorance, which can distort and divert the flow of your thoughts and allow noise to interrupt your thinking, making it easy for your ideas to run riot.

You tell someone that you like their outfit when in fact you don't think much of it. You've decided to *believe* you like the outfit when you don't. The confusion weakens your memory and the clarity of your thoughts, and you gradually lose sight of what you really think.

False appearances, deceptions and lies: no matter how trivial they may seem, it's smarter to refrain from accumulating thoughts based on incorrect information.

DON'T FORCE OTHERS TO LISTEN TO YOUR IDLE TALK OR GOSSIP

Out of the four precepts on speaking, abstaining from engaging in idle talk may be the toughest one to understand. It includes all types of idle chit-chat, along with a desire to rattle on that will make you talk so much you'll end up talking about things you didn't mean to mention, which isn't to anyone's benefit.

When someone talks continuously and forces others to listen, the energy generated by their klesha for desire is invigorated and makes it scream to be heard. But what exactly does idle chit-chat mean? And what, by contrast, are meaningful words?

It's fair to say that the Buddhist view of idle chit-chat refers to anything that isn't meaningful to the listener. For example, smiling and saying to the person who made your dinner that the meal was great may be meaningful. It isn't right to lie or to lavish excessive praise. But it's certainly appropriate to offer positive words and bring good cheer, since conveying the message that you appreciate the efforts of your host and enjoy the company of your fellow guests is meaningful from the standpoint of communication.

You can also talk about essential topics with another person that might help them become a better individual or ease any confusion they may be feeling due to disturbing emotions such as desire, anger or uncertainty. If a joke can make someone relax, then that, too, can be a good way to communicate.

Idle chit-chat can be words that aren't beneficial to others or approaches that force people to respond when they aren't interested. You could be bragging about yourself, supplying seemingly never-ending bits of information that others don't need to hear, going overboard with social niceties, or gossiping. The irrelevant information will leave a mark on the listener's mind and increase the noise that disturbs their thinking while also creating lasting duplicates of useless thoughts that take up space in the speaker's mind.

Refrain from being driven by the klesha of desire to feed idle chit-chat to others. Watch your tongue, and it will lead to beautiful, elegant mannerisms. You will no longer need to expend energy on idle talk or the kleshas of desire or uncertainty and will have more room to focus on what is genuinely essential.

THE JAPANESE DISEASE OF SAYING THANK YOU TOO OFTEN WILL DISTORT THE MIND

It feels good to say a heartfelt *thank-you* to someone when you're truly happy or glad, or when someone is expressing their sincere gratitude to you. But, as I said earlier, it's quite stressful to say something if you don't mean it. It's exhausting to express your gratitude to someone when you aren't feeling grateful, and the person you're saying it to will see through the emptiness of the gesture.

But we Japanese are fond of saying *thank you*. Countless books and ingrained beliefs tell us that we can be happy if we always say *thank you* in our mind and live with a sense of gratitude.

People who believe that will try to say a silent *thank-you* in their mind at any cost. If you say it regardless of whether you're upset, under attack or in a situation where any average person would get angry, the inconsistency between the look on your face and the words coming out of your mouth will create a disturbing, unbalanced impression. You're lying to yourself when you try to express gratitude when you don't mean it, and it can only skew your mind. Being stuck in a state of self-persuasion and repeatedly saying *thank you* without conviction will make people think that it's a habit of yours to say *thank you* when you don't mean it.

In Buddhism, we believe that there are only four emotions that we should nurture in order to live happily: kindness, compassion, joy and equanimity.

1. Kindness is the virtue that wishes for peace and tranquillity for all living beings.
2. Compassion is an emotion of sympathy, wishing to eliminate problems and suffering in others.
3. Joy is the ability to see others who are happy and to feel the same pleasure.

4. Equanimity is a peaceful state of mind in which you eliminate the habit of feeling anger or confusion.

These four emotions do not include gratitude, however. I think this is because gratitude isn't something that you must make an effort to feel. A sense of gratitude is generated within us when something nice happens unexpectedly. In Japanese, the word *arigatai* means 'a state of being thankful'. It consists of kanji characters that represent 'a rare occurrence'.

You are unlikely to find anything in Buddhist scripture where Buddha says thank you to express gratitude to his apprentices or where he's apologizing. Instead, there are positive evaluations – that so-and-so is doing well, for example, or making splendid progress. It's the same for the apprentices. They don't seem to thank Buddha in scripture, either, though they make positive remarks, such as how they have received enlightenment thanks to Buddha's guidance and have begun to see things for the first time.

MODULATION AND VARIETY ARE NEEDED TO EXPRESS GRATITUDE

I'm not saying that you shouldn't be grateful. The best thing to do when you're genuinely thankful to someone is to express your sincere gratitude. And it's best not to act in the same way when you aren't truly grateful. Making a clear distinction here will make you more aware of when you are feeling gratitude.

Particularly in a corporate setting, there may be times when people expect you to show your appreciation to them. I'm not suggesting that you refuse point-blank to do so. What you should do is offer it in moderation. As with excuses and simple apologies, it's best to avoid repeating false words of gratitude or making excessive compliments.

To properly convey your gratitude to someone, it's easier to communicate your feelings by increasing the variety of words you use rather than repeating *thank you, thank you, thank you*. Let's say someone gives you something to eat. Be descriptive. Instead of merely saying or writing those two words in a note, tell them how you enjoyed the delicious taste or how everyone in your family enjoyed it.

Instead of saying *thank you*, which everyone does, give some thought to choosing the words that best describe your reaction. The more effort you put into coming up with something unique and original, the sharper your mind will become. Think about what it was that the other person did or said that made you happy, and you'll continue to expand the lexicon of words at your disposal.

What should you do when you receive something that you don't like? Lying and forcing yourself to tell them that the food they gave you tasted delicious not only increases your stress level, it's also inconsiderate. They may believe you and give you the same thing again, which would be a waste of time, money and effort for them.

It's best to stick to the facts. An honest response such as *'It's been a while since I ate mushrooms'* would be smart. You could also make specific suggestions for what you might prefer another time. Suppose you're sorry to be incapable of appreciating the gift. In that case, you could blame yourself, saying you have never acquired a taste for the item, instead of making a direct apology.

Breathing

While people often say you should breathe from your tanden, a point below your navel, or breathe deeply and relax, the way to breathe is not the most important thing to note. Speaking for myself, I don't tend to use different breathing methods in my meditation. I think the important thing is not how you do it but rather the effort you make to focus on the activity itself.

Let's think about how we breathe in everyday life. We will be short of breath if we're irritated, upset, agitated or excited, or if we're trying to force someone to do something. Our breathing is slow and deep when we're relaxed, and it's short and sharp when we're nervous.

When we meditate for a while and start to focus on our breathing, we become aware of how shallow our everyday breathing has been.

We may be talking with others, having a meal or working. When we turn our attention to our breathing, we will become aware that it is very shallow when we're frustrated or trying to impress others. It will dawn on us that we can't continue to strain ourselves in this way. Once we realize the strain that we've been putting on ourselves, our mind will automatically make the necessary corrections for proper breathing.

We change when we realize that there are issues with our image.

We change the way we speak when we realize that our speech is awkward.

We change our mindset when we notice a distortion in how we think.

By becoming aware of the discomfort of shallow breathing, our breathing will start to change. Once our breathing is comfortable and even, the negative emotions linked with strained breathing will go away. The desire to boast or to reproach others will begin to weaken.

As you focus on your breathing during meditation, it's possible through practice to notice the different emotions that pass through your mind. By doing this, it will gradually feel more comfortable to become aware of your feelings. In the same way that you observe others, read their faces and understand their behaviour, by focusing on your breathing you will develop the ability to spot the signals that determine the direction that your mind wants to take. Practise observing your emotions as you focus on your breathing during meditation and your breathing in everyday life will eventually adjust so that it is no longer strenuous but in sync with your mind.

2. LISTENING

Buddhist meditation is essentially the practice of using the state of concentration achieved while meditating as a tool to observe the movements of one's mind. We may hear the sounds around us as we focus, which may prompt our thoughts to wander. Our thoughts will acknowledge the sounds, recognize them and react to those they find unpleasant. We then practise concentrating on the sounds around us and on preventing our thoughts from further wandering so the chain reaction will stop there.

Based on the meditation lessons that I offer, I find that beginners tend to concentrate solely on the unpleasant sounds they start to hear.

An effort to focus only when they hear something annoying is not going to help them.

In this section, we will practise concentrating on listening in order to control the stimulation that enters our mind through our sense of hearing and stopping unwanted thoughts from buzzing around in our head.

DON'T BE 'BRAINWASHED' BY SOUNDS; BE AWARE OF WHAT'S GOING ON

Maybe you've experienced being frustrated, taking it out on something and feeling worse because of the sounds that you may have made in the process. This happens because these very sounds will further stimulate anger within you and lodge in your mind.

It's no exaggeration to say that every day we risk being affected by the threat of being 'brainwashed'. Stimulating sounds and images from television are bound to have an impact on your mind when you are in the habit of watching programmes without much conscious thought. Some things will have a substantial effect and stay in your mind, setting off noises of unconscious thinking. Keep listening to the simple tunes that accompany TV commercials, for instance, and they'll set root in your mind before you know it.

The same applies to words, phrases and slogans that you have heard in the past. They may initially strike you as distasteful, as if pushing you to accept someone else's opinions. But on hearing them repeatedly, you develop the illusion that they were your idea in the first place. That's when they change from 'words that are imposed on you' to 'words that you have articulated'.

It's good to lend an ear to words and sounds when you know they're positive and will guide you in the right direction. But it's dangerous to be subjected to repetitions of the negative without being conscious of their impact on your mind. An example of that is the case of the Aum Shinrikyo doomsday sect* whose members kept saying

* Responsible for carrying out the deadly sarin attack on the Tokyo Metro in 1995.

over and over: '*We will train, we will train, we will train*' and '*We will make offerings of money, offerings of money, offerings of money.*'

When you think about it, it's never a good idea to keep listening to shouts, screams or other sounds of aggression. These are noises that, once heard, continue to irritate the deepest part of your mind. Words of attack rush through your head and leave negative traces behind, accumulating in your subconscious before you realize what's happening, until, that is, something sets them off, so that they rise to the surface and pop out of your mouth.

Besides violent sounds, it's also probable that a person who is continuously screaming at other people will negatively influence you. It's better to distance yourself from individuals like that if at all possible. I hope you will take this opportunity to think about your usual surroundings. If you're raising children, for instance, an environment fraught with shouts, screams or loud noises will have a negative impact on them and cause emotional instability. So it's better not to have fights with your spouse or make a lot of noise in front of your children.

I suggest making it a habit to practise doing things without making a noise. Opening and closing the door, placing items on a surface, using tools – whatever you're doing, try to remember that you're aiming to do it quietly. That way, you will do things more carefully, and your movements will be more elegant.

SHARPEN YOUR AWARENESS BY FOCUSING ON IMPERMANENCE

However, our mind has the habit of wanting to let in intense stimulation. Everyone is good at lending an ear to words of flattery, for instance. Indeed, I'm sure we all listen attentively when someone's telling us how wonderful we are.

Let's say we're standing inside a building. We're very good at listening to any unpleasant sounds outside because they are incredibly stimulating to our senses. And because of that, we will continue to be aware of them and it may affect how we behave.

If we look at this another way, we can say that we are unable to focus on less stimulating sounds. One example is the sound of a clock. We rarely pay attention to the clock's ticking at home during the day, and because the world is full of potent stimuli, our mind chooses to ignore such muted sounds. But once we stop doing whatever it is that we do and get into bed, our mind then prepares to rest and the amount of stimulation it receives lessens. Because there is less stimulation, our mind then begins to look for more. That's when the ticking of the clock starts getting on your nerves.

It isn't as if the sound of the clock will go on for ever; you know you'll stop noticing it eventually. But you can't help listening to it at that moment, and your mind acknowledges the frustrating stimulation, telling you how noisy and irritating it is when you're trying to get to sleep. Indeed, before long your mind will become bored by that stimulation and stop focusing on the noises around you, forgetting about the sound of the clock. It will now turn its attention to something more stimulating – the things that concern or worry you, from little things such as wondering if you'll be able to get to sleep and wake up on time the next morning to more serious concerns about your life. Your mind will now start to wander, hoping to find more significant worries that will stimulate it. By that time, tiny sounds like the ticking of your clock will have disappeared from your mind completely.

Let's consider the possible ways to escape from this type of situation.

From the time we get up in the morning until we retire at night, we hear many sounds. The majority of these sounds will not stimulate your kleshas of desire or anger. Maybe the sounds that you hear during your daily commute are dull. Perhaps you couldn't care less about the conversations that people are having aboard the train. You can't engage with this sort of background noise, and you try to ignore it. Many people try to distance themselves by listening to their favourite music on their iPods, thus stimulating their kleshas.

But by making this a regular habit, you'll strengthen the impulse to reject sounds that appear uninteresting to your mind, encouraging it to replace them with exciting sounds that stimulate it in a negative way. A simple routine like this – blocking out ambient sounds by listening to music – will condition your mind to always search for stimulation. Your mind will learn that it merely needs to reject uninteresting sounds that bring on little stimulation yet are detrimental to your ability to concentrate. Make it a habit, instead, not to rely on sounds that are highly stimulating. Be alert. Don't ignore your surroundings. Lend an ear to voices and other sounds that do not stimulate your emotions of desire or anger. Instead, try to generate a neutral feeling inside you.

Here is one way to practise focusing on a particular sound.

You're standing in a room. It's filled with the noise of people bustling around. Look out of the window and notice the wind. You probably haven't done that because you've been tuned in to the sounds around you. Once you focus on the subtle sound of the wind, you may be surprised to learn that it can stimulate your mind in a positive way.

Keep focusing, zoom in on the sound, and your awareness, which has been suppressed by the various noises immediately around you, will be revived and you will be left feeling refreshed. The reason why the sound of the wind had earlier seemed boring is because distractions had dulled your awareness. Pay close attention to similar details, and you'll notice that things are continually changing. Everything created in this world continues to change at a breathtaking rate, and nothing is permanent. That's what 'impermanence' means.

We go about our daily lives, preoccupied by things that stimulate us in a negative way, and we aren't aware of subtle, more satisfying forms of stimulation. But as we become aware of the minute changes of impermanence and learn to sharpen our awareness to keep up with its speed, we can gradually hone our sense of perception and achieve a deeper sense of satisfaction.

OPEN YOUR EARS TO THE SOUNDS OF THE WORLD AND YOUR WORLD WILL CHANGE

Because the modern world is so full of stimulation to our sense of hearing, we often tend to become desensitized, even to conversations that are moderately stimulating.

It shouldn't be difficult to listen to your boss or a colleague at work because the office is an inherently stimulating environment, and you know that you should listen to what they have to say. Yet the stimulus of your workplace isn't enough, your mind starts to wander, and it ends up with a mix of unneeded thoughts perceived as internal noise.

Let's say you were listening to your favourite music on an iPod right before you started talking to someone about your work. Your unconscious is already hesitant at that point. It's vigorously entertaining the thought that you don't want to listen to monotonous sounds or voices that don't interest you, and it isn't easy to conveniently switch to a state in which you can focus on the conversation about work. You've been listening to great music until that point and rejecting the boring sounds around you and so, naturally, it will affect the conversation you have with the person in front of you.

On the other hand, if you've been paying attention to all the subtle sounds around you before starting the conversation, you'll be in a focused frame of mind and ready to listen carefully to what the other person has to say. You won't have to pretend that you're listening but will do so automatically. You'll concentrate on the conversation fully and understand what needs to be understood.

Be it the sound of a person's voice during a conversation, the voices during a meeting or the sounds made by birds or the wind, it isn't wise to focus only on a brief moment and consider that the end of the sound. According to Buddhist belief, everything is connected or interdependent. Everything happens because of the connections that exist beyond the flow of time and through individual interactions – what is known as 'dependent arising'.

So if you want to communicate well with your significant other, you should listen carefully to what the people at work have to say. If you want to communicate well with the people at work, you should listen carefully to the sounds you consider offputtingly loud and noisy when you're in town or the sounds you find boring and monotonous during your commute.

And if you want to develop the ability to open your ears to such subtle sounds, you should pay attention when your loved one wants to talk to you, and so on. Everything affects everything else and is part of an interconnected whole, like the stars that make up a constellation. Don't discriminate between those stars. Give an equal amount of attention to every one of them, and the world of the sounds around you will become enriched.

COMMUNICATION BASICS: OBSERVE THE SIGNALS OF PAIN RELEASED BY OTHERS

When interacting with others, we're often overly preoccupied with what the other person is saying. It isn't as if everyone is a professional speaker. As only a handful of people can talk about things that interest the listener, you may naturally find some conversations boring if you're focusing solely on what they're saying.

Here is an example. Your significant other is complaining about work. Maybe it's boring to you, but it isn't as if your loved one wanted to tell you about work in the first place. They want to gain your understanding. What's most important when you're on the receiving end is **to see and accept the person's emotions.** Focus on things other than what they're saying. Note the pitch of their voice, the speed of their speech and changes in their breathing.

Focus first on the sounds, and you'll realize that interesting changes occur in quick succession. His or her voice might become high-pitched and nervous or suddenly switch to low and relaxed. The fast, furious speech might become clear and precise.

Due to a lack of stimulation because the topic appears boring, our mind turns on the command to ignore what they are saying. Instead of listening, we end up thinking about other things (unless the person speaking is someone new and exciting and therefore stimulating to our mind).

But the more observant and perceptive you are, you will start to notice how the person's breathing and their tone of voice can change in a flash. You will have begun to understand impermanence, and with that in mind, their complaints about work will no longer be boring to you. Indeed, what they say will start to become very interesting.

Continue to strengthen your observations, and you'll be able to observe how the level of suffering fluctuates in your loved one. For example, when he or she starts to pause with a meaningless *'Uh'*, *'Um'* or *'Well'*, it means their concentration is breaking up. Their mind is in a state of confusion from their attempt to process irrelevant information while they speak. When someone starts pausing like that, you can tell yourself that they're confused. Don't interrupt or try to rush them, but just settle down, listen and observe.

There are also times when they may halt, take a moment to breathe and then suddenly start to speak in a rapid-fire manner. Those are signs that they are experiencing a strong sense of bitterness. Or they may not say anything after taking a breath. Maybe they want to say something but can't manage to say it.

The same applies to a person whose voice suddenly becomes higher in pitch or who suddenly starts chattering or begins to sound harsh.

A person who tends to hold back their emotions will not want to acknowledge their anger. Because of that, he or she may suddenly start to speak politely or in a flat, monotonous tone. Since it will be clear to anyone observing that the person is suppressing their anger, the words will not be perceived as pleasant, however. Forcing yourself to put a lid on boiling emotions simply will not work. It isn't possible to sound calm when that doesn't reflect what you have inside you.

Our emotions also continue to change in an instant. A person may stare at you, or they may avert their eyes, and their facial muscles may be either tense or relaxed. Whatever the case, take a moment to observe these small changes that signal the person's distress. When you begin to supplement those little things with understanding, you're likely to develop a genuine interest in them and want to do something to help alleviate their pain.

Because we aren't sensitive to the distress signals that people send out, we often ignore their cries for help. We may even add to their burden by making an offhand remark, such as that they're repeating themselves. Or we may become annoyed that the person is making a habit of complaining to us so they can feel better, and that stress will add to our anguish – when in reality they're not feeling better at all. They may be having difficulty breathing, their facial expressions distorted with pain and their voice sounding uncomfortably high-pitched.

All miscommunication between individuals is based on the delusion that the other person is experiencing emotional relief, if not a sense of pleasure, at our expense. We can brush aside that veil of delusion by focusing our attention on the information that comes from that person – the sound of their voice, for example – and realize in the process that what they are expressing is nothing other than the pain that they're going through. Only then are we able to feel compassion or a sense of mercy for the person.

Once we clear our mind and stop having unnecessary thoughts, we enable ourselves to pay close attention to each titbit of information we receive, however trivial it may seem. We will usually perceive such information as intriguing. Our mind will learn that this is how our emotions can gradually settle down to a peaceful state. As a result, we will be able to concentrate on conversations that may not seem very stimulating. Challenging ourselves to manipulate our mind in this way will produce unexpected benefits.

WHEN CRITICIZED, LOOK FOR PAIN IN THE ONE WHO CRITICIZES AND GIVE YOURSELF ROOM TO BREATHE

Making a habit of focusing your awareness on the sounds that a person makes will help you stay calm when they say something negative, such as when a colleague criticizes something you've done. You'll be frustrated enough as things stand if your work isn't going well. At that stage, the disturbing emotions in your subconscious are already on the move, making you angry and upset that things aren't going your way. Negative words of criticism when you're in a state like this will only fan the flames and make your dejection worse.

You may become angry at the person for their words, prompting more uncomfortable emotions to accumulate inside you. But remember, although you may feel as if you're getting back at that person by criticizing him or her in your mind, you're the one who will suffer as a result.

To stop hurting yourself with the poison that we call anger, you must stop processing information when it comes into your head. The moment you start to feel uncomfortable, make an effort to push your thoughts back to where they were before the information first began to come in, and think. You're becoming emotional simply because sound waves have hit your hearing. You must now analyse and clearly define their sound types. Based on real information such as tone and pitch, explore what lies behind the words the person has said to you.

First of all, remember that **pain or stress is likely to be prompting them to say those words**. They're acting that way because they want to relieve their pain by criticizing you.

However, note that it won't help to tell yourself that the person is only saying those terrible words because they, too, are suffering. You won't be able to convince your mind unless you have a real sense of the evidence that supports their pain. Rather than listening absently to their negative remarks, it's wise to pay as close attention as possible.

If they are criticizing you in a grave voice, and it sounds as if something has caught in their throat, it means energy from their klesha of anger is behind their criticism. Because anger is stimulating their brain, they will misread the situation, feeling good to have that stimulation. But, in reality, the person is being guided by their klesha of anger. It's making them hurt themselves with the poison of anger, adding to their pain.

Or they may appear euphoric, clearly enunciating their words while making nasty remarks or criticizing you, sounding deliriously happy. That type of frenzy where they're looking down on others comes from the klesha of arrogance. People feel excited when the klesha of arrogance stirs up their mind because of the release of a neurochemical that functions in a similar way to adrenaline, leaving them exhausted once the sensation wears off.

By taking a moment to stop your thoughts in this way and carefully observing those sounds, you'll be able to find the pain that the person is experiencing. When they say something unpleasant, stop and analyse the information before you as you look for the source of their discomfort. You'll be able to give yourself breathing space by understanding that they are suffering pain on a subconscious level.

By making a habit of careful observation and analysis, you'll learn to deal calmly with unpleasant situations without increasing the anger that is trying to build up in your own mind.

THE PRACTICE OF STOPPING MANIPULATIVE INFORMATION FROM ENTERING YOUR MIND

The steps I have just discussed are for those moments when you hear something unpleasant that makes you feel uncomfortable. Naturally, a better way is not to feel uncomfortable in the first place. For that, you need **to practise stopping manipulative information from entering your mind**, so that the information is not then processed subconsciously. It's the practice of regularly focusing all your attention on the act of listening, and stopping your thoughts from wandering.

Whether they are pleasant sounds that stimulate your various desires, unpleasant sounds that make you angry or monotonous sounds that touch on your klesha of ignorance, you should accept those sounds as they are and obtain as accurate a picture of them as possible. I'm not saying you should take the words themselves at face value, rejoicing, for instance, when someone flatters you. Just remember to concentrate on the sounds as they are.

It's a deep-rooted response in us humans to feel happy when we hear nice sounds, to be depressed by unpleasant sounds and to ignore sounds that we perceive as boring. We become acutely aware of the sounds around us when we get into the habit of analysing whether they're pleasant, unpleasant or neutral. As a result, we do less and less *thinking* in response to something that's said to us, and our mind doesn't overreact just because someone has made a nasty remark.

Once we start to break away from the habit of instantly responding to sounds and learn to remain calm, we will be able to acknowledge that those sounds, whether pleasant or unpleasant, are simply stimulating our sense of hearing.

It's essential to be aware that words of praise will bring you joy and hard criticism will bring on a sense of depression. Being prepared to expect such a mindset will allow you to respond more rapidly. Particularly with feelings of anger, you can stop your emotions from firing up if you brace yourself before you're seriously irritated. Quietly say to yourself, '*Uh-oh, one more word from that person, and I know I'm going to start feeling depressed.*'

Take a moment to stop and rally your thoughts while waiting for the other person to speak, and be prepared. Anticipate the sounds that will make you happy or unhappy. The important thing is to direct your attention to your own emotions rather than what you think the other person will say.

Here is what Buddha said in a sutra called the Mahali Sutta:

A person who listens to a voice and produces impulsive energy like anger or desire will lose subjective control.

His mind will be preoccupied and obsessed with the story.

The story of the different types of stress brought about by the voice will be amplified, and his anger and desire will damage his mind.

A person who accumulates such damage will become a stranger to peace of mind.

Buddha also said in the same sutra:

When subjectively listening to a voice through the sensors of the mind, a person will neither resist nor be a slave to his desires.

His mind will not be captured or obsessed with the voice.

By listening or accepting a voice in such ways, the damage to his mind will disappear and no longer increase.

Smelling

There are times when we're travelling by train or standing in a lift and we find it impossible to ignore a smell emanating from the person next to us.

But rather than overreacting to an unpleasant smell, we should try to be like Buddha and maintain control over our mind. We can allow these smells to exist, acknowledging that it's down to our mind being irritated by odours that stimulate our sense of smell, as in the following example:

Your frustration increases because you're annoyed; your anger increases, accumulating negative karma; then you acknowledge that it's only a smell and stop overreacting.

Our sense of smell is quick to react, and it also acclimatizes quickly to the stimulation. It responds quickly and gets numb, which means getting used to something will make it easy for us to lose interest and for our klesha of ignorance to get to work.

Although we may have an acute sense of awareness of other people's smells, our own smell tends to be familiar, and we become insensitive to it. It's the same as getting used to the distinctive smell of our pets or the interior of our home. Stop at your door the next time you're away for a few days and check and see what it smells like inside the moment you open it.

It's the same with bad breath. The Japanese word for anger is ikaru. It is written in old Japanese using characters that also mean cutting the stomach, suggesting that anger can cause damage as if cutting the stomach with a knife. People today, who suffer a lot of stress, often have bad breath caused by hyperacidity. It often goes unnoticed, but it's vital to check if you have bad breath and to address the underlying stress, such as by practising the techniques for focusing on sounds covered earlier in this chapter.

If you like wearing perfume, I suggest using diluted essential oils extracted from natural ingredients like grapefruit or lavender instead of chemical fragrances. As for incense, I recommend natural scents like sandalwood or the aromatic wood agalloch. It's important to try to control the odours emitted by your body as much as possible by rethinking your diet if needed.

As a vegetarian, I've noticed that the smells of my own body – my breath, body odour and the pungency of my stools – are becoming less and less strong, which is one reason why I suggest considering a vegetarian diet. You can still eat meat but dilute the smells of your body by reducing your intake and balancing it with more vegetables.

3. SEEING

There is an increasing number of different types of things today that stimulate our vision. If people from before the Meiji era (1868–1912) were to see the vast array of movies, television programmes or video games available to us now, they would probably stare open-mouthed in astonishment without taking in the content.

It's preferable, however, not to allow into your field of vision items that are overly stimulating. Once you become used to such an intense level of visual stimulation, you'll be able to focus on other things that stimulate you, such as the face of someone you're meeting for the first time, but you'll lose interest in less novel items, such as scenes in nature or people you see regularly, and will be easily distracted. What, then, should you look at, and in what way? Let's take a look at *the practice of seeing*.

STRONG IMAGES CAN FEED OUR DISTURBING EMOTIONS

I can say clearly from a Buddhist perspective that it's preferable not to look at things that arouse anger or cause your mind to be confused. Isn't it better to look at a clean room than a messy one, or to view a quiet scene in nature than a big crowd of rowdy people?

I'm not a strong advocate of television and other visual media that provide intense stimulation. Violent films, even the news, cover adverse incidents that can be disturbing. Variety and comedy shows can also be offensive. People get hit, smacked, made to do things they don't want to do, even if it's just an act, and then ridiculed. The audience laughs: that in turn triggers their aggressiveness, their anger and their klesha of arrogance.

We sometimes laugh when someone makes a surreal remark, which sounds funny because the information it conveys doesn't connect in the usual way. Things that would never happen in real life are linked and generate humour. When we continue to receive information of this kind on an unconscious basis daily, our conscious mind will start to get confused. It will have trouble connecting recollections, and start believing that ideas we've heard from other people are our own ideas. It will strengthen the tendency to nurture ignorance.

From a Buddhist standpoint, I suggest **making a strong effort to look at things that have a neutral impact rather than those that arouse desire or anger.**

One example is when you're walking along a street. Don't ignore the scenes around you. Pay particular attention to how the small details in your field of vision change while you're in motion. Make a conscious effort to look at the things around you instead of merely seeing them responsively. Once you start to do that, you'll begin to *see* that there are many things nearby that you may have previously ignored. '*I see a sign now. It's coming up closer. I've passed it, and it's now out of my field of vision.*' You will see the usual scenes that you previously considered boring in a new light and thereby boost your power of concentration. As you become more acutely aware of the little things that most people overlook, your attentiveness and sense of perception will deepen, and your mind will be clearer.

It's best to avoid paying attention to things that inflate your ego. Examples of this are the emails on your mobile phone or computer, payslips that tell you how much you make each year or bank statements that show how much you have in your savings. Looking at things like this will negatively stimulate you. They may make you feel good initially, but the klesha of arrogance will eventually surface. Your desire to win people's recognition and your belief that you deserve it will be harmful to you in the long term. At the same time, you may also be shocked by the realization that you aren't as popular or as well off as you would have liked. That will fan the anger inside you as well.

The mind tends to look for short-term pleasure gained through stimulation. It's easy to succumb to stimuli that will make us feel good for now, but such actions will be detrimental in the long run.

It's best to keep to a minimum the things we see that we know will affect our sense of pride or self. It's wise to resist the impulse to keep looking at such stimulating items.

MISCONCEPTION: 'I'M SUFFERING, BUT THEY AREN'T'

As I've been mentioning, it is essential to look at other people during a conversation. It's not just good manners; by taking note of a person's facial expressions as they speak, you'll be able to detect what kleshas are guiding them or see their pain. Though they may not express it directly in words or actions, any klesha of anger or desire that may be present will inevitably surface and, most significantly, be revealed in their facial expressions.

The key thing is to look at their eyes. Are they downcast, and does the person appear unsettled? Are they looking directly at you? Have they suddenly started to fidget nervously? This indicates that the noise of their thoughts is preoccupying their mind. A glance in another direction or a look clouded with emotion indicates the emergence of some klesha.

Something else to note is the person's facial muscles. Are the muscles in their cheeks tense? Are they sporting a fake smile as if attempting to hide something? Are their brows furrowed? The creasing between a person's brows often appear without him or her being aware of it.

It's important to note the expressions on a person's face because these are accurate reflections of what is going on in their mind. You can tell when someone feels pain, even if they don't say it. Once you start making these observations, you won't ignore the subtle changes during a conversation, which signal that you should change the subject under discussion.

Body language is also essential to observe. Such movements may not be evident when a person is focusing hard during a discussion. But their body language will become more significant when that concentration is lost, and their posture will start to slacken. Playing with their hands, moving their fingers, fidgeting, stretching – all of these point to the emergence of a person's kleshas, making it difficult for him or her to carry on the conversation.

Have you had the experience of talking with someone, and the conversation doesn't seem to be quite in sync with their body language? You'll be able to see the pain that's overwhelming them if you're observant, allowing you to react immediately by getting things back on track. If you can see the signs that indicate that the person is in pain, you'll be able to generate feelings of compassion in your mind to help ease the other person's discomfort. On the other hand, if you continue speaking in the same vein, oblivious to their suffering, they will start to look bored and make negative remarks until you finally become aware of their pain.

But people tend to get angry when they become aware of the other person's pain. What an attitude – not listening when you're speaking to them! How rude! You see the person as the aggressor and yourself as the victim. You're suffering, but they aren't. But in truth, it's the other person who first started suffering. Try to understand that they're the victim, and the anger, the annoyance that you feel about their attitude, and the desire to go on the offensive should begin to dissipate.

DON'T GIVE YOURSELF FEEDBACK ON YOUR OBSERVATIONS

What's most important when observing the pain in another person is to be objective, which means not allowing the emotional impact of your observations to fill your mind.

For example, if someone looks bored when they listen to you speaking, you'll tend to think that they're bored because of you. But constantly worrying about what others think of you reflects the klesha of arrogance. Don't give your emotions feedback on the other person's reactions to what you're saying. Look at it this way: if the person isn't paying attention to you, it means they're in some kind of pain. Make it a habit to think about how you can reduce that pain for them. Please don't allow yourself to be disappointed in that person because they're ignoring what you say. Be objective. Think about the approaches that you can take to reduce the pain. Changing the topic or the way you talk may help. Don't be tempted to provide feedback to your klesha of arrogance, which wants to be recognized and accepted, or your klesha of anger, by vowing that you will not forgive the person for not bothering to listen to you.

But it may not be possible to respond as you should straight away. If you have an important presentation coming up and want to stay calm in the face of a mixed response from your audience, the trick is to do what you can without worrying too much about winning over everyone. It would be nice to awe everyone with your presentation, but if that isn't possible, one way to cope is to allow those who look bored to fade into the background. Some will pay close attention during your presentation, and others will be doodling on their notepads. Focus on the people who look interested. Watch them and see if they appear to stay engaged throughout your presentation. If they do, it will prove that you have succeeded in carrying out your objective, which will mean that you will have also delivered as intended to others who may have at least some interest in what you have to say.

But if you lose the ones you thought were interested during your presentation? It's best to change the direction you've been taking. The important thing is to avoid focusing on the easy targets. Don't concentrate on people who are rooting for you due to personal connections or who habitually lavish others with empty praise, and avoid those who can't be objective. Otherwise it will be tough to break out of this group and reach others.

However, please remember that the measures outlined here are just suggestions; the main thing is not to ignore reality or people's pain.

Another issue when speaking in public is stage fright. People who suffer from it have butterflies in their stomach and feel uncomfortable. The arrogance klesha invades their thoughts, generating concern about what will happen if they mess things up or if the audience thinks they're a failure. The result can only be a negative evaluation by the audience. Like those speakers who worry unduly about the audience getting bored, **these types of people give too much thought to their relationship with those in front of them.**

If you're prone to this way of thinking, take a good look at the person or people you meet, regardless of how many there are in front of you. Try to be objective and take a moment to look at the expressions on their faces and see how they behave. Observe. Imagine taking a step back and zooming out for a broader view of them and their emotions, so that you have a bird's eye view of the whole. And I repeat: do not give your emotions feedback on your observations.

PRETEND YOU'RE BUDDHA – CONCENTRATE WITH YOUR EYES HALF CLOSED

Many of you have probably seen images of Buddhist statues with their eyes half closed. These deities aren't looking at anything in front of them. They're in the process of creating a state of total concentration.

There are two ways to meditate, either with our eyes completely shut or half closed to narrow our field of vision. As seeing requires a great deal of energy, we close off our vision, either in full or halfway, to develop our ability to focus. When something happens, and you feel that you're about to lose your composure, close your eyes to shut out everything in sight and concentrate on the movements within your mind. Anyone can do this to regain control of their mind.

When you're upset or feeling nervous, simply close your eyes and focus on your breathing until you can regain your composure. If your mind threatens to go blank while you're giving a presentation, don't be afraid to close your eyes for a moment and concentrate on your breathing. The noise generated by the thoughts that emerge in response to the pounding of your heart will take over your mind otherwise, making it go blank, and the klesha of anger will rise up and push you into doing something that may make the situation worse.

Please don't think reflexively like that. It won't help to get annoyed, angry or to panic. Stop what you're doing so you can compose yourself and quieten that feverish impatience. You may suddenly forget what you were supposed to say next. If that happens, close your eyes, prevent visual information from entering your mind, and concentrate. Then it will come back to you. It's a mistake to believe that anything can happen if you wish it to happen. That's a klesha, and the harder you try to believe it, the more your head will start to spin. It will go around in circles, you'll lose track of what you were supposed to say next and your mind will go blank.

Don't panic. It's important to stop what you're doing, stop what you're thinking, reset everything, and go back to where you began with a clear mind.

ALWAYS BE AWARE OF YOUR FACIAL EXPRESSIONS

So far we have been discussing 'seeing' from our own perspective. But just as we see other people, it means that they are also taking in images of us.

First, be aware that every move we make is being watched by others and affecting them subtly. Most people give themselves feedback based on their observations of other people, and the slightest movement in another person's eyes or face can cause them to relax or make them wary. So, when you're face to face with someone, it's better not to tense your face, furrow your brows, shift your gaze back and forth, or move one part of your body or another when it isn't necessary. Always bear in mind – just a small corner of your mind will do – that when you meet people, they will be looking at you as an image, which will be providing stimuli to their mind.

Let's say you're spending time with your partner and stealing glances at other men or women or shifting your gaze to anything other than your beloved. Even if you don't mean to reject them, they'll feel sad that you aren't paying attention to them and believe that you aren't listening to anything they're saying. It's essential to look at them, concentrate on them and give them your undivided attention. You need to show that you're seeing them.

On the other hand, maybe it's the other way around, and your partner isn't paying attention to you. Don't complain in words. Draw their attention back to you through physical contact. Hold their hand or snuggle up to them. That way, they'll be more aware of you, and it will be easier to bring their attention back to you from whatever is distracting them.

As to friends or interpersonal relations at work, we tend to exchange fewer words and speak more slowly with another person when we're both relaxed. When we feel comfortable with a colleague, it may not be necessary to speak to each other to convey acceptance while sharing the same space. A friendly look or a gentle smile is all that's needed. As long as we know that we accept the other person and they accept us in turn, it can be very relaxing without the need for many words.

Of course, you have to have some degree of mutual trust with that person for that to happen. By being aware that you look relaxed, you'll be enhancing the level of relaxation that shows in your face. On the other hand, while attempting to look relaxed when you aren't will seem contrived and have a negative impact, being aware of how you look will further enhance your positive emotions, making you look more relaxed.

Conversely, we may suddenly look annoyed when we hear something unpleasant. When that happens, don't try to control the tension in your face. Be aware of the feelings of anger inside you at that moment, observe them and let go. It's crucial to make it a habit to be aware of our facial expressions at all times.

Laughing

Kleshas determine the expressions that we see on most people's faces. A smile, in particular, is often used to cover something up. We have a strong tendency to try to protect ourselves when things aren't going well or when we face trouble.

If you think about it, when people are experiencing their happiest moments, they look fully relaxed or wear a gentle smile on their face.

Many Japanese people who do not speak English struggle when approached by a foreigner, and for some reason they laugh. But it doesn't mean they're having a good time. It indicates that they're very nervous and probably exhausted from the effort they are having to make.

A fake smile like that is caused by the klesha of ignorance, to cover oneself up. You want to say it's okay, things are going well, but because there's a mismatch between your mind and the look on your face, you end up feeling stressed.

When you get into the habit of being aware of your expressions, you'll start to notice when your face is tense and gain a sense of the pain that is causing it. You'll realize that it's the stimulation of pain that's making you respond strangely – such as laughing – and be able to stop sporting those awkward, stilted smiles.

On the other hand, remember that there's likely to be underlying tension when a person wears a stiff, unnatural smile on his or her face. It's their pain that's ordering them to put on a fake smile. Make it a habit to look at people in that way, and you'll stop being misled by what they say or how they look.

A person who is laughing is being affected by intense stimulation. A hysterical laugh means they're considerably excited. I think comedy shows on television are popular because people have a subconscious desire to receive stimulation from comedy, which has a significant impact upon us, overwriting our woes and letting us forget about our stress in real life.

I loved to watch comedy shows back when I was living with a lot of stress. But if you think about it, laughter usually seems to be triggered by one of three poisons:

1. A sense of superiority from making fun of the mistakes made by others, or greed (wanting more for ourselves).
2. Emotional identification with the aggressive stance of a comedian on television.
3. Confusion caused by absurd words or actions, or ignorance or doubt.

In other words, comedy can instil in you the klesha of greed (desire), anger, ignorance or doubt if you watch it without thinking. And on television, laugh tracks are added, and in Japan subtitles appear on the screen as if telling people when they're supposed to laugh, pressing viewers to conform to their expectations. Perhaps comedy is associated with peer pressure based on the fear of an inability to laugh when everyone else is having a great time.

It's okay if you're laughing because you're genuinely enjoying the show in a relaxed way. But if you're laughing at someone being ridiculed or in response to the abrasive humour of the comedy act, what *you are expressing is in fact anger you're converting to laughter. You will have a strained expression on your face and your voice will sound shrill.*

If the people around you are laughing at someone (a comedian) and their faces are looking strained, try taking a step back and watching their expressions. You will then gain a sense of compassion for them that they're laughing because of certain kleshas in their mind. You won't have to be the only one who's feeling uncomfortable, and you won't have to force yourself to laugh along with the crowd. Instead, you're bound to feel relaxed, any tension will disappear from your face and be replaced by a faint smile.

Make it a habit to carefully monitor the expressions on people's faces – including your own – and that will allow you to be comfortable. Once you're comfortable, it'll be natural for a gentle smile to appear on your face.

If you ever feel that you're forcing yourself to laugh or that you're laughing too loudly, direct your mind away from the situation towards a feeling of relaxation. Lift the corners of your mouth, just a tad, into a gentle smile. Practise stopping yourself from being swallowed up by intense stimulation without realizing it.

You're attacking someone when you make fun of them and laugh about it, and the same psychology is at work when you laugh at your own mistakes. Though you don't want to make a mistake, it just happens. It hurts your pride, which is frustrating and unacceptable, so you split yourself into two. One half makes fun of you, and the other half attacks you. The moment you think to yourself that it's frustrating, which you don't like, you side with the half that's making fun of you. It's the klesha that wants you to be smart. It makes you want to maintain an image of yourself as a sophisticated individual who can acknowledge the mistake they've made and laugh about it.

In these ways, I think that when we laugh we tend to feed our delusions while simultaneously attempting to forget what's happening. Note also that, when we laugh, the noise coming from our thoughts that urges us to fake a response or make fun of something will also increase.

Always try to be aware of your facial expressions and eliminate unneeded tension so that you can smile gently and comfortably. Allow me to add that it's crucial to calm down our kleshas of desire and anger to avoid smiling in an insincere way.

4. READING AND WRITING

With the development of the internet and email, our communication methods have changed dramatically over the last two decades. The desire to connect with others and be accepted has created a massive market for transactions, involving enormous amounts of money. In this section, I would like to talk about reading and writing, including the internet and email. As you read, please also refer to the 'Seeing' section above.

THE DESIRE TO BE ACCEPTED CAN GENERATE MONEY

As we saw earlier, the ten precepts of Buddhism include an instruction to avoid idle talk. Idle or meaningless chatter, as previously discussed, refers to talk that isn't beneficial to the person on the receiving end or that will oblige them to respond as a social nicety. My feeling is that we're seeing more and more meaningless chatter swilling around in the world today.

Meaningless chatter can be useful at times, but if that's all we have going on, we won't have room to conduct productive or meaningful discussions. While it may not be possible to eliminate idle talk, it might be sensible to decrease it by about a third.

Underlying meaningless chatter is the klesha of greed, in the form of a desire to be accepted and avoid being disliked by others. There seems to be a particularly strong connection between the desire to be accepted by someone and an opportunity to generate money, which applies to mobile phone calls and texts, emails, blogs and online social media in general.

Blogs (or 'weblogs') originally began as a way for people to post on the internet sources for news and other topics that interested them.

Then someone developed software for creating blogs, it became easy to set up web pages without needing to be an expert in computer programming, and a rapid spread ensued. Blogs in the form of diaries became popular, and they eventually became a tool for people to express themselves.

But according to a survey conducted by the Japanese Ministry of Internal Affairs and Communications, less than twenty per cent of the blogs found on the internet are updated more than once a month, which suggests that many people may have begun a blog, found they were unable to continue updating it and so left it unattended.

It's easy to start a blog in the hope that other people will see it. But unless the blog is completely unique or on an intriguing subject, they will not go to the trouble of leaving comments. If people don't respond to what you've written, it is likely to leave you feeling lonely and rejected. Many people will therefore choose to stop working on their blogs to save their pride, and it's wise to bear in mind that these weblogs can feed our kleshas.

Writing a diary and sharing it with the public will nurture the desire to gain understanding and recognition from others, which will lead to the pain of rejection when you see that this isn't happening. Even if you receive just five comments, the pain of wanting to be recognized will disappear briefly, lessening the anguish and making you feel good. But although the pain may have stopped during that moment, it will continue to exist in different forms. You know you have to keep writing well but can't come up with an engaging topic, you aren't sure if you'll be able to write something that will interest other people, those five comments aren't enough and you'll suffer the pain of wanting more comments.

What is the biggest issue? If you were to give a score out of ten for the pain you felt during your initial concerns while writing the first instalment of your blog, those ten points of pain will disappear when people read it and appear to have been replaced by ten points of pleasure. Your mind will then unconsciously register that it has experienced pleasure because of the pain and that the pain of uncertainty and effort is therefore a good thing. It will brainwash you into believing that more pain is welcome if it means more pleasure. What you're doing is going ahead and increasing the pain, or stress, that is of no help to anyone. Because you'll be under the illusion that thirty points of pain caused by doubting if you'll be able to write well will result in thirty points of pleasure when that pain disappears, you will continue to allow the pain to snowball. And eventually, when you can no longer bear the pressure of having to update your content and have people evaluate it, it will come as no surprise that you'll want to forget about your blog.

Then there are the social-networking sites, or social media such as Facebook or Instagram or the local social media service Mixi in Japan. Accounts on social media are not open for public view, and others can't see your page unless you acknowledge one another. While it enables you to become friends with your friends' friends and build your connections, I think the most significant advantage of these sites is that your writing doesn't have to be as impressive as the content of a blog.

While it isn't easy to write intriguing diary entries or articles on social media every day, friends who have registered with you will see what you post and so there isn't the same fear that no one will read what you write as there is with a blog. Because you will know immediately by checking your browsing history whether your friends have been looking at your posts, you can experience the illusion that someone is always reading your content and accepting it to make you happy. For that reason, there has been an explosion in recent years in the number of people who use social media.

But to achieve that experience, there is an unspoken understanding that you will read your friends' diaries and post comments as well. It may seem as though you're making more and more friends when you have an increasing number of people registered with your account, but the larger the number, the greater the pressure on you to reciprocate.

You will need to keep updating your posts, and you'll also have to read other people's posts and make comments. And even if their posts don't interest you in the least, you can't be honest and say you aren't interested, which means you'll have to lie to yourself and start accumulating pain in your mind. That happens because, in addition to not wanting other people to dislike you, you believe that you are not a cold-hearted person who isn't interested in other people's affairs, nor are you a bad person who would lie and pretend to be interested. You're trying not to see who you are.

In Buddhist terms, this klesha of a lack of shame is called *muzan*. It's a movement of the mind that makes you do things that aren't good without a second thought and oblivious to the consequences. Pretending to be interested when you're not and lying to yourself to overlook such self-deception would fall under *muzan*, I think.

DISTURBING EMOTIONS ACCUMULATE WHEN YOU KEEP WANTING MORE

For many years, I have had a website where I provide information about Zen meditation and consultation and am aware of the pitfalls of doing that. How can we use the internet, a very convenient tool, without being overwhelmed by our kleshas?

First of all, if you write blogs or articles, I suggest writing the initial content on a sheet of paper by hand. Don't continue to be connected online. Piece together a draft manually, organize your key points, and then go online and start writing. When typing on a keyboard, which we can do much faster than writing by hand, I think we often end up being controlled by our high-speed thoughts and this will show through in the finished piece. We produce articles on things that we want to write about, and we don't bother refining them. We don't give ourselves the chance to consider whether they will be beneficial to readers.

I think it's a good idea to spend a little more time writing something that is high in quality, has value as information and makes people happy. Let's say you come up with ten topics on which you would like to write. It's sensible to consider and select just three or four of those ten items. Because you'll have extra content to work with, you can eliminate the parts that aren't relevant, so only the most appropriate material remains. Maybe you can't wait to get started, but I suggest making a considered selection and paying close attention to the choices that you've made in the process.

Avoid being driven by your emotions to write things that make you unhappy. Although many people today seem to be using the internet to give bad reviews of movies they didn't enjoy or restaurants they don't like, writing negative things will simply agitate the person who's doing the writing. And in turn, there will be people who get excited criticizing what he or she has written. Maybe they all write hoping to help rid the world of unpleasant things. But all they're doing is doubling, tripling and quadrupling the klesha of anger in their mind, with an increase in stress and a very negative impact on them both physically and psychologically.

It's better to stick to writing only about the films and restaurants you've enjoyed and to offer information that will leave the reader thinking it's been helpful. **Write only about the things you've enjoyed, and never write anything negative.**

When you receive a comment or a response on your website, whether it makes you happy or sad, don't get too excited. Don't start walking on air because more people visit your site or you're receiving words of praise. Think of that joy as a manifestation of pleasure in response to the pain of wanting recognition. Leave it at that, and you should be able to avoid obsessing over results that will only boost the negative kleshas in your mind.

On the other hand, maybe you're getting fewer visitors, or you're receiving negative responses. Don't be upset. It's better not to conduct traffic analysis so you won't have to worry about the number of visits. You can also eliminate the sections for comments and trackbacks. You might as well not have a Q&A section if you're going to be depressed when no questions come in. Encouraging other people to respond and say positive things is only an attempt to satisfy your klesha of greed, a way of assuaging the negative feelings provoked by the pain of wanting recognition.

The stronger your desire to be accepted or to write negative things yourself, the bigger those kleshas will become, distorting your mind. If, when you use the internet, you end up feeling drained and depleted, this is a sign that your kleshas are getting out of hand. To regain control, I suggest that you take a step back and re-evaluate how you use the internet.

ANONYMOUS POSTING ON THE INTERNET MAKES US MORE SHAMELESS

Much of social media revolves around the sense of uniqueness and identity of its users, based in turn on the klesha of greed that makes them want everyone to accept them. Conversely, many posts are often anonymous, with the person's identity omitted. People who make them tend to act differently from the person they are in real life or use a screen name so they can pretend to be someone who doesn't really exist.

Anger can play a significant role in online forums in which people can say what they want without revealing their identity, which can easily tie into a desire to attack someone. The reason for this is paradoxical. When someone doesn't act like the person they usually are, the result will be that their true nature is revealed.

When writing anonymous posts or using a screen name to act as a different character, we believe that we're acting like someone else, and it isn't who we are. Because we're sure that it's only a made-up character, we can attack others online, spread sexual fantasies and delusions or even go as far as to make death threats.

Naturally, we believe that people won't find out what we're doing. But more than that, we don't need to think that we're such a terrible person who would do things like that. It's the klesha of *muzan*, or shamelessness, at work here, in which we lose control by fooling ourselves into thinking that it's a different individual who is doing those awful things online. **The apparent hatred that we express while pretending to be someone else is an expression of the true self inside us that we keep tucked away in a deep corner of our mind.**

When we write offensive words on online forums, the rage this provokes in us stimulates our mind and our brain rewrites that as something that feels good. While we may think that it has helped us feel good and forget our troubles, what has happened is that we have stimulated our klesha of anger, the noise level in our thinking has increased and our pain has intensified.

Pleasure is something that doesn't exist physically. It is an illusion that we experience when our pain decreases and the brain misinterprets the elimination of pain as pleasure. That is the truth that we embrace in Buddhism, the concept that *everything is bitter*. Once we experience the taste of pleasure, we want it more and more, and for that, we seek more pain. And when someone is in agreement with the pain within us, our klesha of greed or desire will surface, stimulate our mind and become addictive. Even when someone contradicts us, our addiction deepens as the stimulation of anger against that person fans our klesha of anger.

As our klesha of anger is affected simply by looking at negative posts, I believe it is wise to avoid them completely.

Most of us today have mobile phones, so we can check how many comments we're getting for our online diaries and the extent that people like them, any time and anywhere. Every time we do this, our subconscious mind receives intense stimulation, like an electric shock. Negative stimulation happens when we see that no one has been reading our posts or fewer comments have been received, crushing our self-esteem and increasing our pain.

In these ways, seeking to fulfil the desire to be recognized by other people is a waste of time and simply feeds our ego. If you are in the habit of checking the amount of traffic or comments you receive on your blog or social media page, I would suggest stepping away from that routine.

DON'T PIQUE SOMEONE'S SELF-ESTEEM, EVEN IN A CASUAL EMAIL

When typing an email, pay attention to writing with care. Read it over and see if it conveys effectively what you mean to say. Unlike speaking to the recipient in person, the advantage of writing an email is that you can spend plenty of time putting it together.

We should remember what we write can also be read repeatedly by the recipient, which means that the impact we make will be significant, whether positive or negative. Angry feelings conveyed in an email will continue to stimulate the recipient for a very long time, if not for ever.

We have time to review and rewrite our emails. Rather than sending an email as quickly as possible, we should note the impact our words may have on the recipient. As in any writing, I suggest drafting the critical points by hand and then typing the email and checking to see if your desire to boast, however indirectly, or your desire to make the reader understand you, doesn't appear too often. Read over your email. Does it contain any traces of anger, as if you are blaming the recipient for something?

Are you asking a work colleague why he or she didn't leave a particular document where you asked them to leave it? If so, rewrite it. Ask them to tell you where the document can be found and leave it at that. Regardless of whether you have the right to ask why you didn't receive the file, it's better to eliminate any suggestions of anger, annoyance or arrogance in an email.

I've noticed that many people seem to start writing their emails with an excuse for not writing sooner. While it will depend on the recipient's personality, I think it could hurt his or her pride just a little. You probably don't mean it, but the underlying nuance is that you're sorry you haven't responded when you know that he or she has been waiting to hear from you. You will be showing the recipient the subconscious image that you have of them: a person you don't mind leaving on their own, someone who can be made to wait.

People are sensitive to changes in the way others see them. Whether or not the recipient had been waiting for your reply, they may feel a little irritated, objecting to being thought of as someone who has been made to wait.

The decent thing to do is **to try as much as possible to avoid piquing their self-esteem**. It's impolite to start an email with the main topic you want to discuss, and when I feel the need for a buffer, I generally talk about the weather or current events. I do not add subjective views when I do that – I don't say it's depressing because of the continual rain or the freezing cold. I make it a rule to write only the facts. I might say I'm writing this email in a room where it's starting to get warmer after the rain and ask how the recipient is doing, that the clock has just struck noon or there is a full moon in the sky. None of these words have much meaning to them, but they're only greetings. I think it's nice to avoid stimulating the recipient needlessly at the beginning of an email.

As for text messages on mobile phones, many people are prone to measuring their love or friendship with others by how soon they receive a response to a message or whether they receive a lot of messages. Maybe they're in the habit of constantly checking their phone. Be careful not to start stimulating yourself visually by checking your mail notifications, being disappointed if nothing comes in – which is also stimulation for your mind – and wasting time going through your messages. I suggest controlling the urge to check your phone for messages and consciously reducing how much you do this. If you can't do that, it means you're already addicted, so go ahead and let the shock hit you, then make an effort to drop that dependence.

OBSERVE YOUR EMOTIONS BY WRITING A JOURNAL

While writing emails or posting online is undoubtedly a handy way to set out your thoughts, for the observation of your emotions I recommend writing a journal that will only be read by you (that's what the purpose of diaries has always been).

Diaries posted online for public view are not only useless in helping us see our true selves; they can also skew our perspective. It's okay if you can write about yourself objectively without trying to make yourself look good. But most people will elaborate and exaggerate, hoping to make themselves sound intriguing to others and omitting anything that may be detrimental to their image.

When writing a journal, I suggest being completely honest and writing about your emotions in the real sense of the word. Rather than simply saying you were irritated today, include the details as to why you were irritated. Maybe you became annoyed at such and such a time for a specific reason, but then your mood improved about an hour later when something happened. Jot down all the details.

I'm not suggesting that you get carried away and write that you would like more than anything for that terrible restaurant to go out of business. Be objective and write instead that you were irritated and wished that restaurant would go out of business. A diary isn't an avenue for letting off steam. It's a record of the emotions generated by the experiences that you went through.

If it's too much trouble to write all the details, simplify. You can rate the level of your emotions, alongside a brief record of what happened during the day, such as *mild anger*, *moderate anger* or *furious anger*. For example:

I felt annoyed while I had lunch with so-and-so, and he made a sarcastic remark to me. [moderate anger]

Open your diary and read it after some time has passed. You'll be able to see the transitions in your emotions objectively over the past six months or year, and it will eventually become easier to manage them.

I'd like to note that it's very refreshing and feels good to write to someone or receive a letter now and then, particularly now, when you can do almost everything online.

Planning

*In order to continue to do something, it's important to plan. Planning requires thinking, so some people may think that it's the opposite of what this book is saying, **not to think**. But by creating a plan at the outset and following it through, you will need to spend less time thinking about this, that and the other thing, which will have a positive effect on your mind and body.*

For example, let's say you were thinking about writing an email. Before you get started, you glimpse some interesting news story online and start reading – and before you know it, forty minutes have passed. You feel a little tired and go to the kitchen to make yourself a cup of coffee. After finishing your coffee, you come back to your computer irritated that you aren't following your schedule. You start writing your email, but you aren't in the right mood. Not only does it take longer to concentrate, but it's also turning out to be a terrible email. Sound familiar?

People's moods can improve or worsen, depending on whether things are going as planned. That's why it's sensible to get started in exactly the way you want. But why is it that that doesn't always happen?

It's because of the presence of our desires. We delude ourselves into thinking that it will feel good to allow our desires to sway us. But, in reality, it will make us unable to do what we need to do, while the buzzing of our thoughts in our head will be telling us that we should be doing something else or remind us that we still haven't done that other task, and the total amount of pain will be magnified. To avoid this and to accomplish what you set out to do, I recommend the following exercise:

1. *Take time to make a plan.*
2. *Be aware that you will end up feeling bad if you don't accomplish your plan.*
3. *Discipline yourself not to look at things that will get in the way of accomplishing your plan.*

Start by creating a detailed plan. Make a list of the minimum requirements of things to be done within each time frame and establish the most efficient order in which to tackle them. Once you have done this, make a conscious decision not to change that order.

Let's say you give yourself thirty minutes to do Task A. Stop doing it when your thirty minutes are up, regardless of whether you have finished. Don't allow your desire to sway you to do more. Follow your plan and move on to Task B. You can go back to Task A later. Even if you don't finish Task A as intended, it will feel good to know that you were able to follow your plan to stop and move on at the thirty-minute point without slacking off.

The important thing is to create a concrete plan. Make it rational so you won't question yourself along the way, wondering if the order shouldn't have been different, thereby sparking thoughts that start to buzz around in your mind. Give yourself ten or fifteen solid minutes just to plan. Maybe it won't be possible when you're short of time, but it will be less efficient to start working wondering if your plan – or lack of a plan – is satisfactory. A good, well-thought-out plan made at the outset will mean greater efficiency in the long run.

If you want to check the news or look at something on the internet halfway through, include it in your initial plan. Give yourself twenty minutes or so at the beginning and be sure not to go over that. Include a break for a little fun, and above all stick to your plan.

A kitchen timer is a great tool to use for these steps. Not the stop-watch function on your mobile phone or computer, but a simple kitchen timer. A gadget that has other functions will make it easy to slip up. You might make an excuse to yourself that you're going to check what time it is and look at your text messages while you're at it, which will take up more of your precious time.

Once you set up a plan to give yourself an hour to do a particular job, stop thinking about your plan and focus on the work alone until your timer goes off an hour later. That's the way to refresh your mind-set. Follow the rules based on the second point, knowing that you will feel bad if you fail to stick to your plan. It's also important to review what you're doing. If you don't do as you've planned, make a note of the negative feelings that arise as you tell yourself that this is how you end up feeling when you break the rules.

As for the third point, disciplining yourself not to look at things that will get in the way of accomplishing your plan, there are ways to make it easier such as by staying offline when using your computer except when needed or avoiding sites that are likely to tempt you to look at them.

Still, the best way to take control of the sweeping movements of your thoughts is to get into the habit of not looking at what's there. If you're going to write an email, turn on your computer and try looking only at your email account and concentrating only on composing the email.

Don't be fooled into believing that delays and changes are natural or that you can't fight seductive triggers that lure you away from your plan. Stay true to your initial plan and practise maintaining the order you've set without being swayed by your mood. Keep doing that, and not only will you be more productive, you'll also be correcting a habit of your mind to be attracted to things that offer more stimulation. It will help you to be in control. You'll be able to stop your mind from wandering, regardless of the thoughts, desires or anger that may suddenly arise, and get it back on track.

5. EATING

There is never a shortage of products that have to do with dieting: books and DVDs on dieting; health foods and devices for weight loss, and so on. It reflects how most people today tend to overeat, but the true nature of the problem is that people do not eat well. In this section, I would like to talk about ways to practise doing just that: eating well.

THE BRAIN'S MYSTERIOUS WAYS: THE MORE WE TELL OURSELVES NOT TO EAT, THE HUNGRIER WE GET

Why is it that people today overeat? It's because they can't satisfy themselves.

We should be able to achieve a sense of satisfaction if we eat when we're hungry. That's how we're structured. Yet we often eat a snack before we're truly hungry and then eat again at the actual mealtime.

We eat to satisfy our hunger and to enjoy the taste of the food because it relieves us of stress and can make the bad things in life appear to go away, at least for a while. Our blood rushes to our stomach after we eat to help digestion; we feel full and are unable to think too deeply about anything. Indeed, some people probably eat until they're fully sated or even past their limit because it helps them to stop thinking about their troubles. But because of the overeating, they will gain weight and, as a result, they will need to go on a diet. Yet the more you think about losing weight, the more challenging it becomes to succeed.

You were stressed out, eating maybe a little too much to compensate, and now you need to go on a diet. Forcing yourself to stop overeating to relieve that stress will mean losing a way to cope with your concerns. You've got into the habit of eating to relieve your stress. That's why you want to eat so often. But denying yourself each time you want to eat something will only result in a new form of stress.

These denials will add to the stress you've been facing in the first place. And, in reaction, you may start to eat even more in a classic case of diet rebounding, which is not at all uncommon.

The issue here is the direction of your awareness. Once a person starts thinking that they have to go on a diet, they will always think about food. **It's best not to think about food**, but that's what they will always be doing and in a negative way – that they can't and shouldn't eat.

I think that's one of the mysteries about the brain, that the more we tell ourselves we can't do something, the deeper the thought will be planted there, causing us to be more interested in the thing that we can't do. And it makes a profound impact that stays in our mind. And once we lose control, we won't be able to control our explosive impulse to eat.

LEARNING HOW MUCH IS ENOUGH

When you look at things in the long run, severe dietary restrictions are bound to fail. You therefore need to change your approach. As you eat, stop vaguely registering the tastes, textures and flavours. I want you to truly feel and experience the different tastes of the food that enters your mouth.

Chances are, you're probably experiencing less than a hundredth of the flavours and textures. That's because your mind is preoccupied with other thoughts: what you would like to do after your meal, or what a bad day it's been. As a result, what you're tasting is pushed to the background. If you wolf down a bowl of stew without noticing what it contains, pain will arise in your mind because it can't fully acknowledge that you're eating. Next, it will tell you that the food isn't enough, and it will then order you to consume more. Continue to eat like that, and you'll form a habit of not taking in information.

Take your time to chew and taste without simply swallowing everything, and start to appreciate the different sensations. Then you'll be satisfied with the moderate servings that your body needs. It will become natural to eat less, and you will start to lose weight. It will be easy as you won't have to deprive your mind by force or put a strain on it.

In this section, I would like to introduce you to the practice of spending time eating small portions. Since communication will often be the purpose of eating a meal with someone, distracting you from focusing on the food, I suggest trying it when you're alone. The weekends are a good time to eat simple meals of just brown rice and steamed vegetables and to spend plenty of time tasting the food and giving your stomach a rest in the process.

EATING WITHOUT THINKING

Lesson 1: Being acutely aware of your every action

You need to take action to put food into your mouth. Don't move any part of your body without thinking about it. Be acutely aware of what you're doing. Focus your attention on the movements of the muscles of your hand before reaching for your bowl of soup. Once you do, be aware that you're touching it. Now focus in the same way on your fingertips as you reach for the spoon. Feel the weight of the soup in your spoon as you bring it to your mouth. Feel the texture of the soup when your tongue comes into contact with it.

Instead of swallowing the soup right then, first put that spoon down to where it previously lay. Do the same with your fork when you're eating solid food. Put it down after using it to carry something into your mouth. Don't chew during that action, because if you do, your awareness will begin to break up and scatter in different directions, and you will start thinking, making it difficult to concentrate on eating.

Lesson 2: Paying attention to the movements of your tongue

It's the weekend, and you're sitting at your table with a plate of steamed vegetables and a bowl of brown rice in front of you. To make it easier to concentrate on chewing and acknowledging the flavours and the textures, close your eyes to prevent other information from entering your mind.

Now start chewing. The food will gradually break down into pieces inside your mouth. The broken-up pieces touch your tongue. Maybe you don't usually pay any attention to the movements of your tongue, but once you do, you'll notice that it is always in motion. It's moving around inside your mouth, moving and mixing up the pieces of food, tasting it, feeling the texture.

There's a tremendous amount of information there, which is usually omitted from our awareness as we're usually thinking about other things while we eat. But we're now focusing on the details. We're aware of what we're eating and how much of it we want to consume, the nutrition intake, and more. Our tongue perceives information from the textures and flavours, but it usually goes unnoticed, drowned out by the noise of our thoughts.

Stop and pay attention. The tip of your tongue is in motion. Where is it now? What did it just touch? Now it's moved. Feel it. You chew while the food goes around in your mouth, biting it up and breaking it down. The food becomes smooth and thick. The flavours change, as do the textures. Try this exercise by following the movements of your tongue.

The same applies to drinking. Don't drink without thinking. Be aware that you are drinking, that you have just drunk something. It's okay if you're a step behind. Maybe you've realized that you've just swallowed something without being aware of it, in which case you can say to yourself 'Oh!' as you become aware.

If you're tuned in to the information that continues to change from moment to moment, you'll be too busy to think about other matters.

As you continue to practise eating and drinking with heightened sensitivities, you will gradually start to take in the fine details of reality that have previously been overlooked and discarded. Zoom in on that information when eating your meals. You should start to see that happiness and fulfilment do not depend on what you eat or how much you eat and that they are determined solely by whether your conscious mind stops to focus on your food.

Cooking

When eating, the thing to remember is that you shouldn't eat foods prepared in a slapdash fashion. You are likely to want to savour a meal prepared thoughtfully, so to eat correctly, a rule of thumb is to cook with care. Also, cook with care for others, and you will have a positive impact on those who observe the preparations.

The trick to cooking with care is to prepare the ingredients quietly. Although one tends to associate food preparation with the chop-chop-chop sounds of vegetables on a cutting board, the pressure from that action crushes the plant cells unnecessarily. Slice your vegetables by gently inserting your knife at either the top or bottom of a vegetable, then pushing and pulling smoothly as you cut through it. That way, you won't crush the plant cells, there will be no needless damage to them or loss of nutrients, and you'll also stop making a lot of noise while preparing a meal.

Also, make it a rule to hold your knife straight. I've seen some people holding knives at an angle when they're slicing ingredients, and it only adds extra pressure to your cutting. It's best to set the ingredient on your cutting board at an angle and hold your knife straight.

Try to avoid making those metallic sounds of pans and dishes coming into contact. Your movements will become more careful, more elegant. And one more thing: don't get lazy about washing your knives and cutting board during the cooking process. Washing and clearing up as you go along will help you to be more attentive to the details.

Organic vegetables, grown without pesticides or chemical fertilizers, are good for the health, and they have plenty of flavour, even when prepared with mild seasonings.

While it's tempting to go for vegetables sold in bulk at discounted prices, buying cheap, non-organic produce means you're supporting a form of agriculture that destroys the environment by killing insects, and I do not recommend this. Some people may see it as self-indulgent to eat organically grown vegetables. But I think it's wise to stock up on high-quality produce that is good for us and full of authentic flavour.

6. DISCARDING

The critical thing to note when tidying up or cleaning your home is to put things away after each use. It's easy to convince yourself that it's too much trouble to put things away when you know you'll be using them again soon, but they're distracting to leave lying around. Your mind will turn to the items and focus on them, processing the information and recalling different things, which means small fragments of noise will start buzzing around in your thoughts. That's why it's best to leave in sight only the minimum number of items needed for whatever it is that you're doing.

Particularly significant for people today are things related to the internet. If you don't often use it, switch the Wi-Fi off at the source. Left on, it will unconsciously remind you that you can go online at any time, causing noises of thoughts to do with email and blogs to arise in your head and preventing you from concentrating on more important things. It may be a bit of a bother to switch on the Wi-Fi every time you want to use it, but I would suggest taking that extra step to create a distinct change of pace.

In a similar vein, you should always have open space in a desk drawer, a cabinet or a closet. Making sure that you don't increase the amount of belongings you have will help create that extra space. It will also reduce the number of occasions where you'll be trying to recall information about each item that enters your field of vision, which I can say from experience is very useful in decreasing the buzzing noise of the thoughts in your head.

Don't own more than you need. This means not holding on to things, regardless of whether or not it's a physical object. In this section, we will discuss the mindset for throwing things away.

THE FEAR OF LOSING THINGS WILL WEIGH YOU DOWN

Let's begin by considering what it means to own something.

The first point is that the mind will have a strong recollection of the fact that you own the object. Secondly, the mind would have a strong resistance to losing the object. When we observe our mind, we should see that ownership consists of these two things.

Before we even consider the fear of or resistance to losing something, we have a recollection of owning the object. Otherwise, we wouldn't object to losing it. We wouldn't get upset about losing something that we don't know we have.

We aren't able to worry about losing money that we don't know we have, and we can't worry about losing a bicycle that we don't know we own. In other words, when we own something, our mind always attaches the idea that it belongs to us, and we don't want to lose it, even if we're no longer consciously aware that we own it. It's like a subliminal manipulation of information in which the awareness of the existence of an object thrives as noise in our thoughts and goes ahead and makes us feel unsettled.

We humans tend to stock up on things we don't need: a book we've finished reading and are unlikely ever to read again that stays on our bookshelf for ever; items we buy on a whim and are unlikely ever to actually use. And the list continues to grow. The impulsive thought of not wanting to lose something is continuously creating a burden in our mind.

Deep in your wardrobe, you probably have a dress or coat that you wear only once every couple of years. Or maybe a toy that you played with as a child. Maybe someday you'll wear that dress or coat. Maybe you'll pull out that toy, look it over and reminisce about your childhood. Maybe someday. That someday may eventually come, and maybe it won't.

In the meantime, even if that someday does one day come and you're able to put your possession to use, your mind will have been holding on to a faint memory of the item. Maybe you will have forgotten about it superficially. But when you see it, it will click right away. That click proves that the object has stayed in your memory database. It means you've continued to think about it in the back of your mind.

And each time you remember that item, you wonder if you should throw it away. But you don't, because it seems to be a waste of a good item, and there may be a chance to use it someday. You make excuses for not discarding the object.

As a result, a sense of tension arises – you don't want to part with the item, and you tell yourself that you can't – and that tension stays in your mind for ever. A part of your mind keeps telling you that you should get rid of it, while another part tells you not to discard such a fine object. You're stuck in the middle of conflicting emotions, and there's no way out.

You have to make excuses for yourself because you also have an honest desire to get rid of the item. Let's face it: we don't want to part with the things we have. We're afraid to do that. Somewhere deep in our mind, we all know that merely thinking about things like that will burden us more. We're aware that the more we fear and are resistant to losing things, the more unsettled our mind will become.

THE KLESHA OF IGNORANCE IS NURTURED WHEN YOU DON'T THROW THINGS AWAY

When we start to accumulate many things that we've chosen not to throw away, our memory database is increasingly filled up, and there will be more and more items that we can't keep track of. Our ability to assess our state of mind, our ability to see our emotions, and our self-control will decline because of all the invisible information we accumulate. We struggle between wanting to hang on to our things and the impulse to get rid of them. It's disturbing to think about such conflicting emotions. Our mind will be in a state of confusion, and when we reach the point where we pretend not to think about it, we may be overwhelmed by an urge to push everything away into a far corner of a closet.

We may want to throw away a letter that someone gave us a long time ago because it brings back bad memories, but we're unsure because it's a reminder of our youth. Because we don't want to think about making a decision, we shove the item in the back of a drawer and pretend to have forgotten about it, telling ourselves that we'll decide what to do the next time we see it. That's a big mistake. **Although we may believe that we've forgotten about the item, our mind remembers it and continues to ponder what to do with it.**

That's a dangerous thing to do. It increases the area of ignorance in our mind, a pitch-dark place in a state of confusion in which we fail to see the light of truth. The more we want, obtain and obsess over things, the more this area of ignorance will expand.

When our obsession with objects becomes so strong that we start to obtain collections of items, our mind will quickly jump back to dwelling on them when we're thinking about other things. It may occur to us that we need more of such and such an item in our collection, making us wonder how much it would cost to buy it.

When our obsessions become intense, we may spend 0.05 out of 0.1 seconds thinking about those items. Keep doing that, and we will lose thirty minutes out of every hour, five out of every ten years thinking about such things, which means we're losing half our life to our obsessions. Increasing our stockpile of items amounts to creating a fog in our mind that makes it impossible to see the view before us, the things that are there in front of us in real life. It's a fog that dulls our senses and slows down our judgement. It makes us lose track of what we should be doing, the right things to do, the types of people we should be with, how we should speak, how we should listen to others, and all the other instantaneous decisions that we make each day.

Why is it that people want to build collections, increase the number of possessions that they have and accumulate more money in the first place? The first thing that comes to mind is that people believe that their worth will increase if they have those things. They feel comfortable having their possessions, believing that those objects will make them more valuable. We can turn around that desire to have something and say they feel insecure without those things, which indicates the perception of pain that occurs from feeling incomplete without them.

The pain that prompts them to believe that they're unhappy and incomplete without those items urges them to obtain those items. The minute they do, that pain will disappear and be replaced with a sense of happiness – until another type of pain emerges, making them wonder what to do if they were to go back to not having those things. A strong sense of either resistance or stimulus occurs, making people deeply aware that they now have those items in their possession.

When a person often thinks about an item, the pain of having to hold on to it will be etched on to their mind and continue to generate a heavy fog long after they have obtained it. And as they continue to repeat that, acquiring more possessions, a negative karma of greed will continue to accumulate. (In Buddhism, karma refers to how the sum of a person's actions, good or bad, affects them in the future, and negative karma can easily accumulate unless they take steps to address it.) A person's desire for their possessions will then grow and change form to other desires, such as the klesha of arrogance.

Whether with a friend, a lover, a work colleague or a total stranger, you will be more demanding. You will want and expect them to treat you in a particular way. **As your desire to accumulate more things grows and mutates into other desires, so your character will inevitably start to deteriorate.**

It's ironic that although you're trying to accumulate things to improve your worth, your personality will become more unstable. Perhaps people who have a lot of money or live in a luxurious residence are sometimes unstable because they always have pain in their mind where the fog doesn't ever seem to clear.

PRACTISE LETTING GO OF YOUR BELONGINGS AND FREEING YOURSELF FROM ATTACHMENTS

By the way, because I don't lock my bicycle when I leave it in our garden, it sometimes gets stolen. Then I think to myself, *'Oh dear, someone's taken it'*, and leave it at that.

Likewise, when I lose some money, I don't panic, asking myself what the exact amount must have been, or feel dejected. I simply acknowledge the fact that I've lost the money and tell myself to be more careful. And if all the money I have were to go up in flames for one reason or another, I would think, *'Oh, it's turned to ashes.'* I'm not suggesting that you burn your money. I'm only saying that I wouldn't feel insecure or sustain damage if I lost all mine.

During my training to quietly observe my mind and to maintain its clarity, there came a moment of epiphany: I realized that I had changed. I had a genuine sense that the fog in my mind had cleared – the fog that was making me afraid of losing my things. Since then, I feel little, if any, pain in my mind at any time, an equanimity that I believe will remain constant if I misplace or lose something or have it stolen. It's as if there's a bright ray of light shining in my mind, with barely a cloud in sight.

Whether we're aware of it or not, we don't want to lose the possessions we acquire. That's precisely why I recommend throwing things away intentionally as an effective way of training the mind. However you choose to do it is acceptable. You could sell your possessions if anyone's interested in buying them, or you could give them away if the recipient is likely to use them. Or, you could simply discard them like rubbish.

It will be apparent to you when you take action. The long-held belief that you would feel more secure with more possessions around you will prove to be a mistake. You will experience a renewed sense of clarity in your mind, feel stable and secure, and it may become easier to look into and across your mind. You may even feel invigorated in your interactions with others.

UNBURDEN YOURSELF FROM THE EGO-INFLATING THING CALLED MONEY

When you think about it, making a donation is a way of parting with your possessions, doing away with an item (money) that you hold fast to in a most meaningful way.

Money is something that powerfully stimulates the self. We unconsciously believe that we're secure because we have such and such an amount. We're aware of its value, and we want to keep building it. We want to do that because we can trade money for an array of things.

The more money we gain, the more items in the world we can own. That means an increase in the items that we can subconsciously keep within our control. Money is a tool for expanding our reach globally, so it has strong ties to the stimulation of the self.

I think Japanese people today are reluctant to spend the money they have accumulated for purposes other than their personal use. Philanthropy is perhaps more common in western countries, with the very wealthy donating vast amounts of money to churches, charity or for the common good. While engaging in charitable donation on the one hand, some of these rich people may also be taking part in activities that inconvenience others, and perhaps in a sense it's hypocritical. But by extending their reach through the accumulation of karma towards something meaningful and by giving – or parting with – a portion of their wealth, it's possible to prevent one's pain from building further.

While this may sound a little extreme, a person who has parted with ten billion dollars is fundamentally in a better state than someone who continues to hold on to it. Naturally, it's better to use that money for a meaningful purpose than to throw it all away.

The fact of the matter is that the klesha of greed that emerges, and the negative karma that accumulates as a result of holding on to something, will only increase the pain in your mind. Try to see objectively that this is what's causing the state of your mind to deteriorate, and by parting with your possessions, you'll be able to rebuild your karma in a positive way.

One thing to note is that volunteer work and fundraising activities can stimulate you. You're being useful and deserve to be appreciated. And once someone appreciates you, you will be giving a significant boost to your self-esteem. It's like a type of insider trading in self-evaluation. Although you don't receive money for your actions, your klesha of arrogance boosts your evaluation of yourself as a beautiful person who spends money on or works for others without monetary compensation.

Maybe there's only a tiny morsel of desire there to be nice to others. But no matter how small that morsel is, you have to go ahead and be nice, or you will never grow as a person. Even hypocrisy can be sufficient, as long as you keep it under control.

In the same way that your performance in a sport will worsen if you use the wrong training methods, an obsession with self-evaluation will inflate your ego. I recommend staying alert at all times, so you aren't swallowed up by the klesha of greed or arrogance, and making it a habit to take action, not from the mind but from the heart. That's the way to practise doing away with negative karma and nurturing a heart of compassion.

By throwing away your possessions, your personality will gradually take a turn for the better. I don't mean this from a social perspective. I'm speaking from a Buddhist standpoint, suggesting that you distance yourself from your kleshas.

Parting with items, throwing them away, will clear away the fog of the fear of losing something that lingers in your mind, and it will nurture a brave mindset that assures you that, whatever happens, you'll be fine.

Buying

We've now discussed refraining from increasing your stockpile of unnecessary items and parting with things you don't need. It's important not to buy items indiscriminately.

But discount stores are increasing in number, and many people appear to be buying items in bulk, not because they want those items but because they believe it's excellent value to shop at such low prices. Perhaps the items are very low-priced. But if you buy them in bulk, they will still be costly. The main problem here is that you may not need those items in the first place. Buying things at discounted prices when you wouldn't want them at their regular rates means you're lowering the bar for your shopping needs.

Say an item that usually sells for twenty thousand yen is available for five thousand. That's a fifteen-thousand-yen discount – a great bargain, right? Not necessarily. More often than not, it's just an illusion.

When you see a product on sale and feel that you have to buy it, stop for a moment and think. It's only a reflection of the noise from the thoughts in your head that are saying (a) the product is cheap, and (b) you have to buy it because you love great deals. Your desire to buy is only a reflection of your acknowledgement that the product is cheap. By slowing down and assessing the situation rationally, you'll be able to prevent unneeded purchases.

I'm not suggesting that you hold back on all expenditures. You should devote an adequate amount to building a foundation for living your life and spend the remaining money on entertainment and things that you enjoy while refraining from investing in non-essential goods or extravagant items that stimulate you. Don't get your priorities wrong and waste your money on those things you know you don't need, which can leave you with little money for food or essential goods.

The question of what to buy ties into to whom you want to give your money. Try to give your money to people who put their hearts into carefully making good-quality items rather than those who mass-produce inferior objects. Pay the conscientious producers and help them make and sell even better products. There is an angle of investment involved when you buy things. Choose items that you honestly think are good, buy them with the sense that you are paying the people who are making them, and you'll feel good that you're using your money in the right way.

You aren't buying something because it's cheap or because you want it. You're buying the items that you genuinely need in small quantities. Maintain that position, and you'll succeed in distancing yourself from greed and continue to live your life with a positive mindset.

Waiting

People today aren't very good at waiting. Whether we're waiting for an appointment at the hospital or a train that's behind schedule, or a person we're meeting is thirty minutes late, we immediately become restless and irritated. But there's no point in being agitated in a situation like that. Wouldn't there be a significant difference in your mindset if you could spend that thirty-minute delay quietly and peacefully rather than in a state of anxiety and full of frustration?

You can use the time to practise the art of not wasting time. I recommend meditating. Indeed, one of the biggest things that I have achieved since I began meditating is the calm state of mind that I can *maintain when waiting in a long queue or if someone suddenly butts in front of me. You can meditate at any time, anywhere, whether you're waiting on a station platform, for instance, or on the train itself. You will feel calm and refreshed by concentrating on your breathing. If you can't continue to focus for prolonged periods, try chanting a mantra for compassion. Close your eyes and say quietly or think without vocalizing: 'My mind will be calm.' You will not allow the noise that enters your mind to overwhelm you. Maybe someone will shout, 'Oh God, another accident?' or 'There are always delays on this line!' But you will not allow your mind to be swayed.*

If you're on the train itself, you could also turn your attention to the sounds inside or outside the carriage that you're in and practise concentrating on these, or try to sharpen all five of your senses on the things around you.

One way to control your attention before you start to feel overwhelmed by an avalanche of different thoughts is to observe the people around you. Use the thirty minutes to watch the person in front of you as his hands begin to tremble with impatience, or his brows start to crease, and quietly note to yourself that elements of discomfort are now surfacing. That way, you won't have to be irritated yourself or allow your thoughts to wander.

When you begin to properly acknowledge and accept the time that goes by during delays, you will no longer feel that your time has been wasted, and you will always have a sense of fulfilment.

7. TOUCHING

Although the word *touch* may tend to call to mind what we feel with our hands – specific objects or individuals with whom we are intimately connected – those aren't the only things that we touch. We're constantly in contact with what is immediately around us – our clothes, the ground, the air and various sensations within our body. Let's turn our attention to the things that we touch with our body and consider this from a Buddhist perspective, using it to nurture our ability to concentrate and to observe.

PAY ATTENTION TO YOUR SENSE OF TOUCH WHEN YOU LOSE YOUR CONCENTRATION

As we go about our daily chores, we should also be aware of the things that touch our skin: our fingers as they touch the keys on a computer keyboard, for instance, or our bare feet as they touch the floor.

When sitting in a chair and working for an extended period, we start to feel uncomfortable and to lose our concentration. When that happens, focus slowly on the sense of touch between the seat and your bottom, the backrest against your back and any discomfort you're experiencing. If your legs are sore or your back aches, focus on the areas that hurt, and you will realize that your body is tense or your posture a little awkward. Just as we adjust our speech when we become aware that we're speaking clumsily, so our posture will improve. But we won't be able to change if we aren't aware of the tension in our body.

So the first thing to do is turn our attention to the little things, the small sensations of touch that we don't usually think about. That's an essential step in controlling our mind.

I'm sure there are things besides work that can distract you at the office. You have to communicate with the people around you, and the phone is always ringing. You need to coordinate your schedule with your colleagues, and you must also think about what the boss has to say. There's so much noise around you and so many things to think about. Sometimes the burden on your mind can be too much.

A quick way to block out the noise is to focus on the different senses of touch that your body is experiencing. Be absorbed in a single action, and you will be able to go back to concentrating.

One way is to focus your attention on the sense of touch at the tip of your fingers where they are in contact with your computer keyboard. Don't proceed without being aware of this sensation of touch. Consider the touchpoint between your fingertips and the keyboard as your focus area. By focusing your concentration on work you need to do, the noise around you will be blocked out and any stray thoughts lingering in your mind will be less likely to wander around aimlessly.

You will have a vague sense that something is touching your fingers. That sensation is in the background of the task at hand. Bring it out of the background and focus on that sense of touch. You've just hit a key on the keyboard, and you're working the muscles in your arm. Be aware of those realities. Let your conscious mind stop and feel the sensations. Let it gain a steady awareness of the sensations that had been vague up until then.

Then the unnecessary noise in your mind will start to disappear, and you'll be able to focus on your work. That concentration will sharpen your awareness. You'll be able to focus on the bare essentials of the task at hand, and that concentration will in turn sharpen your senses.

If you've lost your concentration and nothing seems to help, I suggest moving away from your desk and taking a slow walk around the office or your study if you're at home. Concentrate on something other than your desk work. Anything other than that activity will do – tidying up, filing, cooking, gardening. Focus on the objects that your fingers or your feet are now touching, and that will decrease the thoughts that are occupying your mind and make it easier to concentrate.

Think only about the bare essentials – your hands as you hold a broomstick, the way you push that vacuum cleaner – and your mind will stop thinking about other things. Touching something while moving your body will both stimulate and relax you very effectively.

TRY TO STOP SCRATCHING LIKE MAD WHEN YOU HAVE AN ITCH

As the second step for honing our sense of touch, the aim is to maintain a steady mindset that isn't affected by external factors such as the weather.

Take a hot summer day as an example. The sensation of heat stimulates the brain, and the shock from that makes you feel uncomfortable. You then turn on the air conditioner. This sequence of events is something that we engage in without much thought. In the short term, it makes sense to cool your body so you can feel better. But in the long term, it becomes a habit for your mind to fix by force anything that it doesn't like.

We're conditioned to understand that all we have to do when it's hot is to eliminate the heat, that by changing that factor, by turning on the air conditioner or removing items of clothing, we can try to become comfortable. And by repeating that, we become intolerant of the smallest things. In other words, our mindset becomes selfish in the long run.

So unless the heat or cold is so severe that it could be physically damaging, we need to have a mindset that doesn't automatically react in this way. What then becomes necessary is an effort to observe and accept. Observe that your body is now feeling hot and perspiring; don't deny it, just accept it.

There are bound to be many other habits and activities that we initiate without thinking. Do you scratch your head or play with your hair? Scratch your nose when it feels itchy? Not scratching an itch immediately is an effective way to practise self-control. Pause for a moment before you scratch.

As I write, a mosquito has landed on me and, for the last couple of minutes, it has been sitting at the base of my thumb. I'm not tense because I'm focusing on the sensation of having the insect on top of my skin, and, in turn, the mosquito seems to be relaxed because it isn't worried that I'll swat and kill it. Since I'm not tense, the mosquito is in no hurry to bite and poison me.

Getting back to the human perspective, people tend not to like mosquitoes because they expect the bite to be itchy. Information on itchiness goes to the brain, which then processes that information as something very unpleasant. Then our mind perceives that as a nuisance – before it even happens. Turn that around, and we can say our klesha of anger is manipulating us.

If you are feeling an itch, focus hard on the itchy sensation at the forefront of your five senses. Your mind will then acknowledge that it's just a minor sensation, and the brain will no longer insist that it's something uncomfortable that you must eradicate by scratching. By concentrating on the itch at its source, you are cutting out the 'because' in the '*I dislike it because it's itchy*'. All that remains will be the itchiness.

I think it may be hard for you to imagine what I'm talking about unless you experience it yourself. Please give it a try the next time some part of your body feels itchy.

Itchiness, in itself, is a subtle stimulation that we perceive through our sense of pain. It reaches our brain, which goes out of control as it registers the itchiness, noting it as something very unpleasant that you must eliminate. Thus, you're rewriting that data. That's how the unpleasantness increases. To stop the brain from getting out of control, we need to concentrate on the facts. We must focus on the information about what's actually happening. Once we do that, our brain will stop processing the data of unpleasant itchiness, and then it will no longer be difficult to cope with the itchiness.

When a mosquito bites you, it injects saliva into your body. If you focus on the contact point, your body will recognize the problem and get to work at once to heal you. In my case, it usually takes around half an hour after getting a mosquito bite that I feel cured – without vigorous scratch marks.

Maybe you don't think the way I do and would like to stress that you scratch because there's an itch, and scratching feels good. But let me ask you this: who is happier, a person who thinks nothing of an itch and leaves it alone, or a person who finds itchiness unbearable?

Naturally, the latter feels anger towards that itch. There's a sense of rebellion against it in the mind, which is in an unhappy state, and the prevailing thought is that the itch must be eliminated. This type of unhappiness can also apply in hot or cold weather or to pain, where negative reactions are fed to the brain via physical sensations, which gradually chip away at your peace of mind.

In Buddhism, it is believed that the fewer adverse reactions of this kind you have, the happier you will be. Maybe it's a hot day. But if you focus on the heat itself, your reaction to the heat will start to dissipate in the simple acknowledgment of the information that it's hot. You will then be able to spend the day without those negative emotions in your mind, you will feel comfortable and will easily adjust to different heat levels.

Resting, playing and escaping

We could say that, in Buddhism, resting, playing and escaping are all connected. People rarely feel the need to take a break or go on holiday when they're feeling fulfilled. But they do want to escape when their klesha of anger or desire is making them tired.

It's better to avoid doing things that trigger strong stimuli when you want badly to escape, because it would only numb your senses against the stress you're experiencing and make you feel exhausted, both physically and mentally. We tend to be drawn to strong stimuli when we're irritated, but it's essential to choose something that won't tire you.

The wise thing to do when you have a chance to take a break is to be physically active in moderation to give your mind a rest. If you're taking a short break from working, you should finish what you're doing, then go to the kitchen and spend time making coffee or tea and drinking it or having a meal, slowly concentrating on the flavours as you eat.

If you're going away on a trip, don't choose a holiday where you'll be hopping from one tourist attraction to another. Consider a trip where you'll be able to get the physical and mental rest that you need. Travel with a loved one to a place where you can avoid crowds, take long soaks in the bath, go to bed early and sleep well, and return before you get bored.

If you want stimulation at the cinema, choose an action film over a horror movie, a human-interest drama over an action film or, better still, a heart-warming story that will gently stimulate you. It will be better for you in the long run.

Movies that make people cry are always popular, but all that happens is that they give viewers a chance to let go of their emotions and feel refreshed. In these movies, we are generally shown characters who face a challenging situation to which we respond with the pain of anger. Our response to the resolution of the challenging situation then frees us from that anger or prompts a sense of relief, which means our pain is removed. We misunderstand that release as pleasure and end up crying.

Suppose you're in the habit of seeing movies like this because your mind is unsettled by the pain it receives in everyday life. If that's the case, you will experience a more substantial level of pain as you watch *the film, are freed from the pain and feel relief, or you may form a habit of looking for more intense pain, which is why I don't recommend watching films of this kind.*

I don't recommend alcohol consumption, either. But if you must have a beer or a glass of wine, have it with someone with whom you can enjoy a good conversation, someone who will not make a scene and cause you to end up arguing. Keep your stimuli moderate and get plenty of rest. Otherwise your brain will only be under the illusion that you're having fun while recovering from fatigue when, in fact, you'll end up feeling more tired.

8. NURTURING

As a final exercise for doing away with needless thoughts and for controlling your mind, let's think about nurturing a compassionate mindset while also nurturing yourself and others. Cultivating a compassionate outlook is the best way to support others and to calm the noise that comes from our thoughts.

Do note, however, that there is no shortage of false compassion in the world today. If you see someone in need, you feel that you should help, which may seem as if your mind is demonstrating kindness when it actually is nothing more than a reflexive response to your thoughts.

I recently heard about a friend of someone I know who mentioned at his workplace that he wanted to leave his company. The people around him quickly got together and held a meeting to hear him out. They offered him a wealth of advice, which should have helped him reconsider, but because everyone went ahead and said what they wanted to say, he ended up feeling as if he was being put on public display and felt exhausted afterwards. This person had probably been sending out a silent call for help at the office. But no one had noticed it or tried to help him, yet the moment that he expressed his wish to leave, he found himself surrounded by his work colleagues.

It shows how a person who becomes weak or wretched can lure others like bait as an ideal means of bolstering their own ego. Helping someone overcome their predicament will often take a back seat to the noises in their mind that scream and fill their thoughts with the selfish desire to feel good.

DON'T BOMBARD OTHERS WITH ADVICE 'FOR THEIR OWN GOOD'

The most important thing that you can do for someone in trouble is to remain quiet – to stay quiet and listen to them talk.

And not in a pushy way. Not like: *'Okay, I'm all ears. Now tell me about your problem!'* What you should do is create a setting in which they'll want to talk. Instead of yakking away yourself, you're listening attentively to what they have to say. Then they'll start to talk if that's what they want to do. The key is to have them settle down, relax and feel safe when they're with you.

Once you've heard them out, remember not to contradict them or agree with them in a way that seems false. The person won't relate to you if you offer them high-handed advice to do something in a certain way. Regardless of how considerate and diplomatic you may try to be, a suggestion to do something differently would amount to telling them that what they're now doing is wrong.

The important thing is **to listen attentively. Give the person plenty of time to talk until the issues they're facing and the things they want are clear.**

That said, if you are to offer advice, you should continue to listen and try to find out what it is that they want to do until you understand their objectives, then you should consider together the possible ways to regain control and to discipline and support their mind. If their mind is veering off in the wrong direction, then think about how they can get back on track. Although you'll still be subtly challenging the person, you would be sharing with them an awareness of what they want or don't want to do and what they're looking to accomplish, and you should not deny their core ideas. Once they start to see the importance of making adjustments, they won't feel that you're disagreeing with them.

Let's say a friend of yours has a general problem, such as wanting to be happy but seeming unable to make that happen. The thing to do is to think about what happiness means to that person. Give them plenty of time to share their ideas about happiness with you. What would make them happy, and what wouldn't? What are the things that are important and unimportant to them? What is it that they want to do, don't want to do? If your friend is contradicting him- or herself, a lack of consistency will gradually start to surface. Listen carefully to the inconsistencies. Give yourself plenty of time to ask that person why they want or don't want to do something. Let them talk through the parts in which they sound confused. To ensure that your discussion doesn't end up merely as a chance for them to vent, I suggest asking questions that will have them sorting through their thoughts to explain things to you. Try to prompt them to be more self-aware and see themselves objectively.

As the two of you continue to talk, your friend will start to see their lack of consistency and consider making corrections, which will result in a gradual change in their ideas about happiness. They won't feel that you have challenged them because they'll believe that they arrived at the conclusions themselves.

If your friend is suffering, affirming everything and saying there's nothing wrong with them will provide only temporary relief. In more superficial styles of counselling, consultations can be more about affirming an individual's ideas. He or she may attend a session with a therapist and achieve a temporary sense of relief, but the distortions in their mind may remain unchanged, and they will not find a fundamental solution to their issues.

DON'T BE CONTROLLED BY THE NEED TO FORCE YOUR OPINIONS ON OTHERS

In any event, you're on the right track if you're able to listen to people's problems. Many people can't do that. They start to talk about their own opinions before listening to what the person with the problem has to say.

Everyone has a subliminal impulse to defeat others and to be acknowledged. When you see someone in a fragile state, you tend to be overcome by the noises of your thoughts that urge you to assert your own opinions without paying attention to what the person has to say. The problem lies in the fact that this happens automatically before you are even aware of it.

We tend to believe that our opinions are correct, and the desire to modify other people's opinions or put them straight often takes over. This desire gains traction when the other person acknowledges our opinion, and it makes us want to insist on our views. Although our fear of alienating them usually keeps it under control, we delude ourselves into believing that we're helping them and that this is the right thing to do. We don't believe that we're forcing our opinions on them. Then we start to lose control.

To prevent that from happening, and as I've said earlier, the thing is to understand how these types of thoughts work. Be aware beforehand that, when you see someone in trouble, your desire to offer your opinion – to help that person out – will tend to surface. If you're aware of that, you will understand how that desire is trying to control you in the background when you set out to offer advice, and you'll be able to figure out calmly that that is prompting you to force your ideas on that person.

It's the arrogance klesha that makes us want to push our opinions on others. We believe that we are helping people in need and are unable to see the harm that we are in fact causing. We should try to maintain a calm mind, so our klesha of arrogance doesn't control us. Focusing our attention on noticing the pain of others is the first step to genuine compassion.

KEEP YOUR SYMPATHY FOR OTHERS IN CHECK

Consideration for others doesn't amount to aggressively doing things for them, worrying about them or sticking to them like glue. Maybe you think it's because you're nice and a good person, but it's also possible that a klesha in your mind is making you nosy. We aren't consciously aware that when our desire to believe we're nice is behind our kindness, we will often be imposing.

When we feel sorry for someone, it may be an emotion based on a sense of superiority. Maybe we're excited about who we are, someone who cares about others, as we bask in our fabulous self-image as a beautiful person. Our mind is thus in a state of excitement as we speak and act, and we aren't thinking calmly or objectively about the other person. Our klesha is making us cling to them and humour them to the point of spoiling them, and although we may think we're doing a good deed, we're not helping them in the long run.

Worrying excessively about others is also quite different from genuine compassion. When someone feels that another person is overly concerned about them, they worry that they're making that person worry. We may believe that we're being nice in worrying about someone else. But if we become uncertain, get emotional or cry when we're with that person, we will feel pain associated with the klesha of anger. It stems from feelings of repulsion, where we sense that the situation isn't right.

For example, someone visits a sick friend in the hospital and starts to cry. The sick friend will not be moved by the visitor's concern. He or she will pick up on the visitor's fears, melancholy and worries and be in a worse mood. At the root is anger, and it will be released in the hospital room, leaving the atmosphere unsettled. That's no way to behave when visiting someone who is sick.

You might say that worrying is like a selfish pastime. You worry because you want to worry. Generally speaking, the more unstable a person is, the more they'll worry about others because it allows them to look away from their own vulnerability. It's the person whom you're worried about that should be pitied, not you. They're the one who is struggling. By worrying about others, people can divert their attention away from their own concerns.

AVOID EMOTIONAL ROLLERCOASTERS AND NURTURE A SENSE OF COMPASSION

From the standpoint of compassion, I've said that it's important to observe others' pain. If you're suffering on behalf of someone else, however, it isn't kindness that you're demonstrating but something that's caused by the stimulation of a klesha.

If a person continues to cry for ever after a family member's death, it may appear to be because of their love for the deceased. But crying non-stop means the person is continuing to feel the pain triggered by the death of the family member and is sending out those negative vibrations endlessly, which certainly can't be good for those who have passed away. Although the surviving party may believe they're thinking of the deceased, they force the deceased to remain in a negative state.

In Buddhism, the best thing to do both for ourselves and for someone who has passed away is not to grieve endlessly but to have a mind of compassion. If we have genuine feelings for the deceased, praying that they are in a calm state as we meditate for compassion – sometimes called *the meditation of mercy* or the *loving-kindness meditation* – is much more beneficial, both to them and to ourselves.

Pray with all your heart that the deceased will be at peace, and you will start to feel calm yourself. Even for the non-Buddhist, contemplation of this kind and acknowledging that the deceased is now free of any pain and at peace, will help you feel calm. A mind filled with grief will be angry, incurring pain, and you will wear yourself out. The only thing that's there is your sadness. You aren't thinking about the person who has passed away being peaceful and no longer suffering. What you're doing is clinging to the fact that the person had lived, rejecting the reality that they are no longer a part of our world, and causing pain for yourself. You're doing nothing more than denying reality.

If you feel sad because you still think about that person being gone, you're not only causing harm to yourself but also releasing anger waves around you. All you're doing is passing those anger waves on to the dearly departed, not to mention the surviving family members around you, which I doubt could help them in any way.

That is not genuine kindness.

You need a mind of compassion to achieve genuine kindness.

People often misunderstand what it means to have compassion. While many people may think it means to feel for others, be sad for them and cry for them, genuine compassion isn't like that. When you're feeling sad for the death of someone you know, you should look for the connection to the klesha that's controlling you and cut it off. You should stop trying to act being kind, drowning in your own emotions and grieving. Once these thoughts are gone, the only thing remaining in your mind will be genuine compassion for the deceased, which will prompt you to pray that they will continue to be at peace.

Say goodbye to the person inside you that likes to act in a friendly manner, and nurture the seeds for developing a delicate sense of compassion. You won't need to endure pain if you aren't a hypocrite, and you'll no longer be causing pain for the other person. Reduce the frequency of occasions where your kleshas control you, and you should be able to achieve a compassionate mindset.

FOLLOW THE RULES, OR ELSE YOUR MIND WILL ATTRACT NEGATIVITY

In Buddhism, there is a term called *zenyu*, which may be translated as *a good friend*. *Zenyu* refers to an irreplaceable friend with whom we can develop our minds in a manner that is mutually beneficial. It doesn't mean in any way that you have to be a do-gooder who hides their true feelings. *Zenyu* isn't that simple, and the concept guides us to stay away from unhealthy relationships. We do not want friendships that will increase our kleshas or be detrimental to our positive qualities as human beings.

That type of relationship will create confusion in our mind. The criteria are very straightforward. Does your mind feel pure and calm when you see people, or does it become confused and agitated at times? When you're with others, the mind will always react in one of these ways, and it's best to avoid individuals who make you feel unsettled.

In Buddhism, this law holds not only for interpersonal relationships but for all things. It applies when you speak, act or think. Will your mind become calm if you speak now, or will it be disturbed? Will a particular thought make your mind calm or pollute it?

If you're on the verge of saying something that may pollute your mind, then stop those words from coming out. Stop any thoughts that may pollute your mind. Stop acting in a way that might do so. These are the rules and criteria of Buddhism. By disciplining our thoughts, words and actions, we can prevent our mind from becoming unsettled.

The same applies to interpersonal relationships. When two angry people criticize each other and are always complaining about the other person, their anger will resonate endlessly and become a device that amplifies their kleshas. On the other hand, a relationship of two good-hearted people will see them influencing each other in a beneficial way and each party bringing their mind towards the other. Their minds will be less polluted and so develop positively.

Zenyu applies to all relationships, which include relationships between parents and their children, between teachers and students, lovers, and colleagues at work, and you'll be able to forge such relationships some of the time, but maybe not always. Since others are always influencing you, it's imperative to consider the individuals with whom you spend time.

Unlike the law, these teachings of Buddhism are not for others to force upon you. You set your own rules, and it's up to you whether you follow them. Buddhism is a way for those who wish to walk that path, and the basis is that *those who come are welcome; those who leave will not be pursued.*

On the other hand, if you don't follow those rules, your mind will be unhappy due to the presence of more kleshas triggered by various stimuli. It's best to observe your own rules if you want to live happily. That's what Buddhist discipline is all about. It's nothing more than the rules you establish and promise to follow to protect your mind.

So even if you don't follow your rules, no one's going to get angry with you, and no divine punishment will befall you. All that's going to happen as a result is that your mind will be pulling in negative things, affecting your ability to live happily.

HOW TO RAISE YOUR CHILDREN WITH ACCEPTANCE INSTEAD OF TRYING TO CONTROL THEM

Children generally grow up being both praised and scolded by their parents and teachers. But when a pattern develops, in which praise is offered if they do as they're told and they are scolded if they don't, children begin to feel that their elders only want offspring who do exactly as they say. They will not acquire a fundamental sense of security of being wanted and will feel very sad.

Children want to receive praise because it makes them happy that their worth has increased. But there in the background is a subconscious sense of sadness that lingers from wondering if their parents don't truly accept them as they are and only want to make their children their puppets.

The way to soften that blow is to let your children do what they want while keeping careful watch over them. If your child is in a challenging situation, it's important to lend them an ear and listen to their problems. Stay calm, don't be overcome by the noises of your thoughts.

If your child is taking exams at school, for instance, avoid over-reacting each time they come home with the results. Don't give them excessive praise when they get good results. Be calm, show them that you're interested and go over what they did right and where they could have done better. Avoid giving your child simple evaluations by merely stating the facts with either praise or criticism alone.

If the test results weren't good, remind them that they scored better last time and tell them that it's interesting how unpredictable these ups and downs can be. Give your child the message that you're interested in them, and they will have plenty of room to grow.

It's easy to say that our children's very existence is important to us. But whenever something happens, we will either praise or scold them, wearing them down in the process. Parents think about the things that haven't gone well in their own lives and try to gain satisfaction by raising their children to be the people they wanted to be. By praising and scolding, we try to gain control.

Attention is essential to show your children during early childhood that you accept them, but don't scold and thus appear to reject them if they scream their heads off. Don't ignore them, and don't treat them like babies. Maintain thoughts of compassion and pray that they will grow healthy and strong as you hold them firmly in your arms and tell them that everything is fine. Such behaviour will build a trusting relationship, which is crucial when your children are very young, between the ages of one and three, when their speech is still in early development.

Always being scolded at that age will create a subliminal sense of non-acceptance. It's the parents' fault if children won't listen to what people tell them to do. Until they've reached the age of three or so, they have yet to develop a sense of logic, so it's the parents' responsibility to make sure that anything potentially dangerous is kept out of reach. The next thing to do in developing a trusting relationship is to show that you're confident. Show them that everything is fine because you accept them unconditionally.

Once your children begin to understand what's going on, you can start scolding them if needed. Because you've already built that trust over the last three years, your children will be unconsciously aware that you are not someone who would deny them without reason. They will have developed the ability to realize that you aren't scolding them for the sake of it and that there must be a reason for you to get mad at them. The first few years are essential for doing this.

Anger management is necessary during the years that follow, as well. If you have a child who likes to make a lot of noise, you could approach them as equals and negotiate. For example, you could say to them:

'I feel bad when you cause a commotion while I work. It isn't because I don't love you; it's because I can't concentrate when it's noisy. I'm a human being who gets annoyed and has bad moods, and since we live in the same home, neither of us wants to feel bad. But if you're still going to make a lot of noise, then we'll need to think of a way to deal with it.

'I get irritated when you make a lot of noise. I'm aware that you may be lonely on your own, but I do need to work for half the day to be productive. If we can figure out a way, I would much rather work at home and with you. Do you think you can help me do that by not screaming and crying?'

You don't want to take a high-handed approach, and you don't want to be too humble with a soft-soap attitude. It's a simple matter of coming to the negotiating table. Whether the issue is between an employee and his or her boss or a parent and child, it's a matter of persuasion – to come prepared with rational options, including things that may not be in your best interests – and to allow the other person to make a choice.

NURTURE LOVE IN ROMANTIC RELATIONSHIPS THROUGH PERSUASION

The same type of persuasion can be applied in romantic relationships.

Let's say there's a woman who would like her obese boyfriend to lose weight. Telling him that she won't love him any more if he doesn't lose weight will have a negative impact on his self-esteem, which is not good. First, she needs to convey to him that her love for him won't change, whether he's thin or obese, and to get him to understand this.

She should then think carefully about the reason why she doesn't want him to be obese. Maybe she feels embarrassed to be dating an obese man because, in today's world, an obese person is considered low in value, and she feels that being with someone like that will affect how she is seen by other people.

As she continues to analyse her thoughts, she may begin to rethink her values and reconsider her desire to be with her obese boyfriend. Maybe it won't matter any more that he's overweight. If not, she should explain her self-analysis in full. It might go like this:

'I like you a lot, but when I think about how other people judge me, I worry that dating someone who is overweight will affect how others perceive my worth. I don't want to be sad because I'm with you. Do you think you could try to lose a little weight for me?'

That might work, and maybe it won't. The couple could get into an argument. Both are aware that obesity could lead to disease, and the man might say he doesn't care if he gets sick. But that is not what they are discussing. It would be useful for the woman to be honest with her boyfriend and better for him to hear what she really thinks.

PEOPLE WHO ARE ABLE TO SUBMIT ARE THE ONES WHO HOLD THE KEY

As the above example indicates, whether trying to persuade someone or attempting to get them to listen to you, it's surprisingly useful to take a look at the movements within your mind and be frank about its distortions. Open your mind for the world to see, and show others the strings that control you. This is akin to submitting or surrendering – the way a dog or a cat might roll over and show their stomach – and it's difficult for someone to continue to resist when their counterpart submits, addressing them with complete honesty.

No one thinks they're a bad person, and no one wants their worth to decline. The klesha of shamelessness makes us feel this way, along with the pride within the klesha of arrogance that makes us reluctant to acknowledge and admit such things. But if we can analyse the things that control us, the impact upon us, and upon those to whom we choose to reveal our thoughts, will be very significant.

As I've repeatedly mentioned, taking a good look at the strings that control your mind will make it easier to control your kleshas because it will be impossible not to change once you acknowledge your true self.

We think about how we walk when we become aware that we're walking strangely.

We think about how we speak when we become aware that we're speaking strangely.

We change the way we think when we become aware of the distortions in our mind.

By recognizing and acknowledging such impulses, people become stronger and develop. But when we're asked if we can control all our kleshas, the answer is that it's difficult. We reflexively close our eyes when faced with something unpleasant. We try to pretend it never happened. We don't see the things we don't want to see. That's the way of negative karma, which continues to accumulate unless you face up to it. Don't be misled by that karma. Be aware of the negative aspects within you and consider opening them up for others to see.

We should have the courage to submit to others. No one wants to lose, and everyone wants to compete. Because of that, we feel as if we'll lose if we submit. But, in reality, the first person to submit is the one who will hold the key for resetting relationships that have become entrenched because of deception all around.

The first thing to do is to say goodbye to the pride that comes from the klesha of arrogance – not wanting to be defeated by others and avoiding showing people the distortions within us. Efforts to discipline our mind will determine whether we can become real friends, be it a relationship between parent and child, teacher and student, or between lovers or colleagues. Those are the efforts that will lead to self-development and benefit those around us.

Sleeping

My final note here is on sleeping. There have lately been increasing numbers of people who have issues concerning sleep.

According to a study conducted by Japan's Ministry of Health, Labour and Welfare, 19.6 per cent of Japan's population is troubled by insomnia. It must be challenging if you want to sleep but can't. But why does that happen in the first place?

As we can see from the large number of people who say they can't sleep due to mental stress, it's because they fall into the trap of a thinking disease. The brain gets out of control. This thinking disease isn't limited to insomnia, however. As we saw in the first chapter, whatever we're doing, whether working, walking or eating, our mind focuses on that particular activity. We're unaware of the noise from our thoughts that echo around in the background. But once we get into bed, our mind is no longer stimulated, the noise that's been hiding behind our awareness begins to surface and the thinking disease takes hold. We seek out new types of stimulation and escape into our thoughts when the stimulation around us fades. We look for disturbing emotions such as anxiety, uncertainty and anger, as these are more stimulating. From that point, our mind will be free to go wild with various thoughts and get out of control, which will excite the brain, and we will never be able to fall asleep.

The large number of people who can't sleep shows how much modern humans are plagued with thinking disease. My feeling is that many people today have fallen into difficult situations because of being led there by their thoughts.

Some people say they eat to satisfy their hunger so they can sleep. Eating will sate you, and blood will flow to the stomach for digestion, and that will relax your mind and make you feel sleepy. Many people consume alcohol to numb their mind, and many appear to be taking sleeping pills.

Perhaps surprisingly, some people watch scary horror movies in bed because they want to sleep and do not want to do any thinking at night. I know people who listen to upbeat music as they doze off. While this may sound peculiar, it might make sense from a Buddhist standpoint since powerful stimulation is one way to numb the existing pain. But when we fool ourselves by using such powerful stimulation, we tend to become less aware that we're suffering from thinking disease.

Blurring our awareness with alcohol, food or drugs will give us temporary relief and make us sleepy, which is a short-term benefit. But in the long run, it will damage our stomach and the rest of our body and get us into the habit of lying to ourselves. What then can we do to go to sleep without relying on such stimuli?

As I have been suggesting, the first approach is to look at every thought that pops into your mind and set them aside in quotation marks. For example, 'I am thinking about [description of the thought].' Observe your emotions and set them aside.

Another approach is to meditate with compassion. In the Japanese language, the word jihi ('compassion') is made up of two characters that translate as 'nurturing' and 'mercy'.

Have a sense of compassion for yourself and focus as you meditate.

By focusing on a particular topic at a time through meditation and by continuing to concentrate, you don't give your brain the room to have verbal thoughts, which are unnecessary and useless. This is a way to train yourself to have only positive thoughts. An advantage of this form of meditation is that your awareness will gradually be directed towards cultivating a gentle, compassionate mindset.

It will be easier to focus on short sentences. For example, if you're meditating to bring yourself internal peace, you can chant: 'May my mind settle down' or 'May I feel at peace.'

When meditating on internal peace, your chant can be along the lines of: 'May my pain go away', 'May my problems go away' or 'May my suffering come to an end.'

Be aware that the violent storms of thinking that so occupied your mind are the thoughts that put you through enormous difficulties in the first place. Be considerate to yourself as you meditate, and you will start to experience a sense of calm.

If a storm of thoughts threatens to invade your mind while you meditate, practise taking note of it at once before going back to your chants.

From the standpoint of making rules for yourself, it's desirable to get up early in the morning, retire early at night and follow a routine. When considering our biorhythm, the four hours between ten at night and two in the morning are essential for rest and recovery, and we should try to go to bed before the clock strikes twelve. Retiring early, getting up as the sun rises and starting the day fresh without any lingering noise from unneeded thoughts is the best part of a Buddhist lifestyle.

III

The strange relationship between the brain and the mind

A conversation between Ryunosuke Koike and neuroscientist Yuji Ikegaya

Born in Shizuoka Prefecture in 1970, Yuji Ikegaya is a doctor of pharmacy and an associate professor in the Graduate School of Pharmaceutical Sciences at the University of Tokyo. He presents academic papers that focus on the role of brain plasticity in the mechanisms of memory. His innovative research, supported by continuous experimentation, has won him many awards, including the Young Scientist's Award; a Commendation for Science and Technology; the Pharmaceutical Society of Japan Award for Drug Research and Development; and the Japan Neuroscience Society Young Investigator Award. His main works include Kaiba *('Hippocampus'), written jointly with Shigesato Ikei,* Shinka Shisugita No *('The Overdeveloped Brain'), and* Tanjun na No, Fukuzatsu na 'Watashi' *('Simple Brain, Complicated "Me"').*

PAIN IS THE FOUNDATION OF THE BRAIN

Ikegaya: I know this is unexpected, but can I ask you a question that might be a little provocative?

Koike: Oh? This is going to be exciting.

Ikegaya: In your previous work, you have written about the importance of silence and recommended the beauty of silence. Why is it that a person who suggests something like that writes so many books and speaks to so many people? That's the first question that I wanted to ask about your stance (*laughs*).

Koike: I see. On the topic of silence, I'm not suggesting that people stop talking. I'm saying we should quieten down the noise created by our thoughts so that we don't end up talking about the loud things that preoccupy our mind when we speak.

We might make the other person feel uncomfortable, or we may think we feel good when we say certain things when, in fact, our body is experiencing pain. I'm suggesting that we refrain from using words that vocalize the loud noises in our head.

Ikegaya: Indeed, you have not written, 'Don't talk'. You aren't suggesting that people stop talking; you're saying we should change the way we talk. That we should eliminate what we call *stimulants*.

I see. I asked my question based on the idea that you weren't talking about silence superficially, with the implication that one should stop asking disingenuous questions like the one I just asked (*laughs*). I understand what you mean.

Koike: That's interesting. I would like to ask you first today about the brain – I feel that in recent years it is being revered as if a 'brain religion' might exist (*laughs*). But I think the brain can be quite a burden on us. For example, there are times when we become angry and attack another person with violent words, and although our heart is racing, our breathing is laboured and our body is becoming exhausted from the effort, we just can't seem to stop. Because the data we're receiving are being converted from *pain* to *pleasure*, we delude ourselves that we're experiencing pleasure when we're suffering. Because of that, we get angry and jealous, which should make us uncomfortable, but we just can't seem to stop.

And although we believe we're thinking autonomously, there's a script in our subconscious that controls us. I think the mind is programmed like that, to convert pain into pleasure, and that induces stress and increases our pain.

In the enlightenment process in Buddhism, you heighten your concentration through meditation to break down awareness into fine fragments. In so doing, you become aware that the stimulation registered in the human mind is nothing other than signals of pain.

It's called *issaikaiku* in Buddhism, an important concept that is commonly translated as 'suffering', 'pain' or 'unhappiness'. The Japanese term is broader, translating as 'everything is pain/suffering'. By becoming aware of this, I think we can say that's akin to putting a stop to the data conversions and rewriting our mind's programming.

The mechanism at work here may have something to do with the brain-processing data, but I'm not an expert on the brain. If the brain is involved in such movements of the mind, wouldn't it be a specific part of the brain rather than the brain as a whole?

Ikegaya: Whether it's structured in that way, we can't say based on the level of scientific knowledge today (*laughs*). But I think that you're correct in considering that negative emotions like pain form the foundation of the brain. I say that because, while the brain is an organ that focuses on the physical, when one looks at it from an evolutionary standpoint, one may see that the brain has evolved in close association with the body.

For example, take the brains of animals like earthworms and leeches. They're more primitive than mammals' brains, consisting of bundles of nerve cells or ganglions, which are similar to the brain, all over their bodies. When we think about how the brain has evolved in these animals, we can imagine that it may have developed as an efficient feedback system. Information from external sources reaches the ganglions, conveying sensations of touch, smell and light. These then decide whether the animal should flee, make an approach or remain still, providing feedback to the body that initiates physical movement. In other words, it's logical to consider that the brains of such animals evolved by converting external data into physical movement.

That's the process of evolution. As evaluation criteria for determining whether to convert input to output, I think the initial values that the brain is equipped with are pain and discomfort.

Koike: The message received says, '*There. That's painful, isn't it? Get moving if you don't like it*', when it gives you a shock of discomfort.

Ikegaya: I think so. In prolonging life, I think it must have been more useful in the process of natural selection to flee from things that were dangerous than to seek pleasure. I mean, their lives were at stake. A system to make you flee from things you didn't like and/or to endure them was probably among the first physiological systems to be created. Evolution ensued, and mechanisms to change discomfort to comfort may have occurred, particularly in the case of human beings.

But this isn't always necessarily the case. You see, mammals and higher life forms are equipped with neural circuits for feeling pleasure. What is known as a 'reward system' within the nervous system gives individuals a sense of pleasure. Phylogenetically, they are circuits that are independent of the circuits of discomfort. Therefore it's somewhat problematic if we say that all pleasure is derived from discomfort. In neuroscience, we can't sum things up with a single interpretation like that. We need to consider that various conflicting factors are at work.

But on the other hand, as one example, I often drink beer, which is very bitter when you drink it for the first time. Coffee's like that, too. When we consider that we like those things, I think it's correct to deduce that people are equipped with a system that changes suffering to pleasure.

Koike: Beer is a toxic substance. You drink it, your body gets excited and prepares for battle, and you don't have to think about the things that had initially been bothering you. Adding a new type of pain enables you to avoid thinking about the things that were originally causing you pain. Believing that that feels good is what I consider to be a processing of information by the brain.

I think the requirements for turning on the pleasure device known as the *reward system* are affected by complicated conditions like that. When the reward system is stimulated, a type of data processing called *pleasure* occurs. But it isn't real.

In other words, when the initial pain is replaced with greater pain, you feel good during the time that the previous pain has gone away. But once you've stopped doing that erasing, the original pain starts to worry you again. Then you get a command that says, '*There. That's painful, isn't it? Do something again to forget it, and you'll find pleasure*', and you might get drunk and say abusive things to someone or blame yourself.

Ikegaya: Harming oneself is an extreme example of that.

Koike: Maybe continual happiness can be found if such a thing as a life that functions on pleasure alone exists, but then you'll think that there's no need to grow because you're always feeling good and relaxed. Maybe it's better to have pain to begin with and to struggle with that.

Ikegaya: For example, when a person's brain sustains damage in the frontal lobe area in an accident, their sense of fear and sense of danger disappear. I've seen patients like that, and they do look happy. Their intelligence is intact, and they understand that they've been in an accident and that their mindset has changed. They say they feel better now and do not want to go back to the way they were before.

But they can't cook, for example. Because they have no sense of danger, they cut their hands when they use a kitchen knife. And they'll keep doing that over and over again and forget having turned on the stove and start doing something else. Without a sense of fear and danger, they're unable to live a basic life. I watch patients like that and feel that we're both lucky and unlucky, as living organisms, for pain to be a prerequisite for survival.

Koike: Pain had to come first.

Ikegaya: Yes. As life forms are designed that way, I think we should accept that as a precondition and start our discussions right there.

Koike: So, the question is how to use that double-edged sword to live a better life.

Ikegaya: Precisely. But unfortunately, it isn't the job of a scientist to answer that (*laughs*). Yet I think about these things because I spend more time living as an everyday citizen than I do as a scientist.

PEOPLE REALLY DO FEEL THE PAIN FELT BY OTHERS

Ikegaya: There's an interesting paper on facial expressions associated with pain. Changes in facial expressions were measured using an electromyogram when people sampled different tastes – sweet, sour, bitter, etc. A unique muscle movement occurred when they tasted something bitter. That muscle, called the levator labii superioris, pulls up the upper lip. In a primitive sense, I think bitterness must have been the perception that people used to identify a poison.

What's interesting is what happens if someone were to see a cockroach on the floor, for example, and grab it with both hands and eat it. Anyone watching that person would squeal in disgust (*laughs*). By taking electromyogram measurements, we found out that people have the same expression on their face as when they taste something bitter.

In other words, aversion may be based on bitterness. In the process of evolution during ancient times, living organisms had already established an efficient system for sensing bitterness, which later tied into aversion.

This experiment can be taken further in a fantasy role-playing game called Ultima, in which money is traded. Let's say that my opponent and I are to be given a thousand yen that is to be shared between us. We can refuse if either of us is not satisfied with the amount we've been allocated, but the game will end if we do, and we'll both end up with nothing. For example, my opponent might complain if I receive two hundred yen and try to take some of the eight hundred he or she has been allocated, but neither of us will win a single yen as the game will have ended.

When you think about that rationally, even a single yen would be better than nothing. But people aren't made to be that rational, and the possibility of rejection by an opponent is approximately forty per cent when the allocations are two hundred and eight hundred yen. Because the one with the bigger share won't accept that their opponent should have more, they punish their opponent by saying they don't want to give them a single yen. It's a social, moral sanction. And when an electromyogram is used for taking measurements, the moment one party feels the allocations are unacceptable, the same facial expressions are evident as when someone experiences bitterness.

Anger, sadness and aversion are the primary negative emotions that we have, and our sense of what cannot be tolerated appears to correlate with the sense of aversion. It isn't anger, where we're rejecting or opposing the other person, and it isn't sadness. It seems to be that aversion related to social, moral sanctions.

When we look back and think about how our moral sensibilities might have evolved, it's interesting that it may have started with the sense of bitterness that animals experienced when they ate something.

In considering correlations between the physical and the social, other intriguing things emerge as well. For example, if measurements are taken of our brain while we are watching someone feeling pain, it's evident that the neural circuits for pain are active, even if we don't feel the pain ourselves.

We might feel sad when we're the odd one out among our friends and experience pain in the chest area. We took measurements of the brain in such a state and learned that the same neural area had been active as when responding to physical pain.

In my brain studies, I feel that it all starts with the physical, such as the sensations of pain and bitterness.

Koike: With linguistic expressions too, words that refer to the physical – for example, 'a bitter memory' or 'a pain in the chest' – are convincing and do not require an explanation to convey the perceptions. For us humans, the physical must indeed be an essential and indispensable part of our lives.

THE WONDERS OF THE CALMING EFFECTS OF FAITH

Ikegaya: An interesting study has recently been published. It's a paper on the placebo effect. A placebo effect is where you take a placebo, or a substance or treatment designed to have no therapeutic value, without realizing that this is what it is, and it works. It may result in pain or itchiness disappearing or a fever going down, though if you are sceptical about it or refuse to believe the doctor when he or she says it is a genuine treatment, it will cease to be effective. To add to that, the higher the price of the medication, the greater the effects appear to be (laughs).

In one experiment, electrical stimulation was administered to the arm to cause pain. A placebo was then applied to the area under the premise that it was a painkiller. The pain disappeared. A study on how the placebo worked showed that the descending pain inhibitory system, which originates in the brainstem and inhibits pain from being conveyed, had been activated.

In other words, it hadn't been an illusion. The pain had been physically blocked. It's the same mechanism as the painkilling effects of morphine, and brain activities went on as if morphine has been administered.

The next step was also interesting. Naloxone is a drug that blocks the effects of morphine, such as in patients who are addicted to drugs. The intriguing thing was that when just naloxone was administered, placebo effects also disappeared. Naloxone is just a chemical substance, yet the physical and the psychological appear to come together when it's used.

An interesting experiment was also conducted concerning stress. There are two types of stress: physical and psychological. Psychological stress is something that you are aware of and are able to express verbally. Physical stress, by contrast, is something that you aren't consciously aware of, although your body feels it. Using modern technology, this physical stress can also be measured.

Let me explain. A lot of physical stress starts in our adrenal glands, located next to our kidneys. The adrenal cortex releases stress hormones, and the entire body gets overwhelmed when large amounts of these stress hormones flow into the bloodstream. By measuring its concentration levels in the bloodstream, we can understand the amount of physical stress a person is experiencing, although they may not be aware of it.

An experiment was conducted concerning physical stress. Pentagastrin is a substance – a poison – that induces physical stress. When pentagastrin is administered as an intravenous drip, the level of stress hormones shoots up. In this experiment, a button had been placed near the subjects' hands. They were told that they could press the button at any time if they wanted to discontinue the treatment. Many of the subjects who had volunteered did not press the button, even when they felt some discomfort. They continued to the end of the experiment, revealing that the availability of the button kept the increase rate of the stress hormones at around a fifth of the rate of those who did not have a button to press. That's an eighty per cent decrease. The subjects with a button should have been experiencing the same amount of physical stress, but the understanding that they could stop at any time suppressed the increase rate of the stress hormones. It makes me wonder what is going on physiologically when we say we're relieving our stress.

I thought it was an interesting discovery that merely having a way to escape the causes of stress would prevent stress from happening, which indicates that physical stress is influenced by the conscious mind.

Koike: You're saying that difficult work today can be fun if you know you're able to quit tomorrow. It's interesting that even in scientific papers we can understand where the physical and the psychological meet.

DO WE HAVE FREE WILL?

Koike: On reading your work, I took note of your comment that while we may think we're moving our arms of our own free will, the brain is issuing a command to move them before our conscious mind decides to do so, and our brain is thereby controlling us, that our awareness has no freedom and we generate the right to revoke these commands when we realize that our brain is controlling us. We have no free will, but we do have the power of veto. As I read that, I thought it matched my understanding very well.

A method that I use for my training in the pre-sectarian or original style of Buddhism [based on the ideas and practices of Buddha himself] is to check my awareness. I try to see how quickly I can become aware of the moment that a reflexive movement occurs in my subconscious in response to something that is predetermined in my mind, before it starts to control me. And for that, it is necessary to concentrate.

For example, I can intercept messages that tell me to be irritated or anxious before they take control. When I focus on concentrating, I can detect whether the commands I receive are useful, compassionate or potentially damaging to me. If I can be aware of them, then I can accept only the beneficial commands.

When we realize that we cannot control our conscious mind, the least we can do is start to be selective, choosing only the beneficial commands that we receive and rejecting the bad ones. And when we continue to do that, it becomes easier for favourable commands to be issued and strengthen the database of information that we have in our mind. That's the concept that I have in any case.

Ikegaya: I can relate to what you're saying, or at least understand parts of it. Because there is no scientific proof of this, I haven't gone so far as to write in my books that positive thoughts will start to come to you, but that's what I believe myself.

There was a discussion about expanding a US base in a region in Italy in 2008. Naturally, a lot of support and objection arose, which led to a referendum being held. A psychologist did some research in the area before the referendum and discovered something interesting.

A week before the polls, a questionnaire was conducted asking residents if they were for or against expanding the military base. Some people said they didn't know or had yet to decide since there was still a week to go before the referendum. But the responses to the questionnaire showed that it was already possible to predict at that point with considerable accuracy whether they would vote yes or no a week later.

Why had that been possible? There are various ways of achieving this, but the one that is easiest to understand is the free-association method. For example, ask a person what comes to mind when they hear the word 'water'. Maybe they'll say 'the sea'. The next item associated with the word 'sea' might be 'fishing', 'fish', 'tuna', 'sushi', etc. In the free-association method, you mention the first thing that springs to mind in a sequence, one after the other.

But this free-association method is curious: I doubt, for example, that many people who hear the word 'water' would associate it with Prince Shotoku, a semi-legendary regent and politician in Japan during the Asuka period [552–645 CE]. The method is supposed to be about 'free' associations, and there's no rule that says you can't jump from water to Prince Shotoku, but if you do, the stages in between can in fact be predicted. The process isn't all that free at all. Maybe some people will say 'plastic bottles' when they hear the word 'water', and others will associate it with swimming. Their thoughts are confined to a particular category. Perhaps we should call it an 'unfree'-association rather than a free-association method (*laughs*).

In any case, I believe the things that people come up with when they hear the word 'water' are reflections of their thoughts. The more we study the brain, the more I feel it's made up of reflexes. By looking at the types of responses that people make when they hear certain words, we can see their thinking habits. And in the referendum in Italy that had been the answer. During the week before the polls, people had watched the TV news, read the newspapers, talked with others and thought about how to vote on expanding the military base. People watched the same news programmes and read the same newspaper articles, but their responses during the referendum varied because they were reflexive, as the questionnaire had revealed. How they voted depended on their usual thinking habits, taking no account of their own free will.

By examining people's reflexive thinking patterns in advance via the questionnaire, it had been possible to see which way they would vote a week later.

Another interesting questionnaire was conducted after the polls. People explained why they voted the way they had and sounded very reasonable, but not a single person imagined that their responses had been reactive – when that was exactly what had happened (*laughs*).

What is important here is the history of these people and the types of lives that they had been living. As experience will rewrite a person's history, they may associate ice with water if another test were to be conducted, as in the second questionnaire, showing a change in their reflexive patterns.

That leads to what you talked about a moment ago about training yourself to ignore bad commands and select only the good ones. As a reflexive pattern, the ratio of good messages to bad will then increase. Although it hasn't been validated scientifically, there is no other way to explain what underpins the development of human values, morals and decision-making. I would like to call it conjecture (*laughs*).

Koike: And the grounds for training to rebuild one's personality would be lost.

Ikegaya: Yes. When we think along these lines, I believe changes will occur by simply having good experiences, being in a good environment or having good people around you. I think these factors may result in reinforcement learning. There's no free will involved, only the freedom to override a command, and most human behaviour is based on the brain's reflexes or reactions. I've been shocked to learn that many people think it sad when I say that. In my opinion, it isn't a bad thing. All we need to do is sharpen our awareness, if that's all we have.

THE MÖBIUS STRIP – SELFLESS ENLIGHTENMENT

Koike: I think you're absolutely right. And when this lack of freedom is thoroughly recognized, in the Buddhist sense, and fed back to the mind, one's sense of self will gradually be demolished. Receiving information, believing it to be a script and breaking away from that perception, which then turns out to be another part of the script – understanding that constant repetition will be a blow to our sense of self. We will continue to feel uncomfortable until we have finally been crushed since our self would thus fall apart. But when that happens, it becomes ridiculous to think that some script is taking us over, and we thus learn to choose our scripts more carefully through the awareness that we are being made into slaves.

When we realize that our mind is but a slave to our brain's reflexes, we can mount a revolution against the things that control us. That is what selfless enlightenment in Buddhism is all about.

You've written that, while it's possible to say that free will does not exist, we can also remain free if we don't know what's going on behind the scenes.

Ikegaya: I think that's very important.

Koike: Buddhism teaches that we will arrive at true freedom when we thoroughly examine the negative sense of a lack of freedom, in a paradoxical loop like a Möbius strip.

Ikegaya: We don't have freedom, but we're allowed to feel that we do. Or we accept without a doubt that we're free, and we live within that illusion. I think the meaning varies entirely depending on how we live. It's like the difference between whether or not you have experienced the Möbius strip.

Furthermore, denying ourselves freedom would lead to the question of whether we're free in the first place, and that would cause more confusion. Still, I think it's completely different between a person who has been through the experience of self-demolition and another who hasn't.

Koike: The mode of reaction would change. Perhaps it's like creating a general design as you look at things behind the scenes.

THE DISADVANTAGES OF
LAUGHING AND THE EFFECTS
OF SMILING

Ikegaya: By the way, you've discussed the topic of laughing in this book, saying it isn't good to laugh (*laughs*).

Koike: I'm not talking about whether it's good or bad to laugh at particular moments, but more in the context of things that become habits in the long run.

I think the more stress that people feel, the more they like comedy. That's because I experienced a lot of stress before going to college and could barely manage to get by without looking for a way to escape reality. I enjoyed watching comedy shows on television and loved to do silly things and play jokes on people. I think a good burst of laughter will give you the illusion that your pain has gone away.

Ikegaya: When people laugh it's said that the impulses carried along the cranial nerves are similar to those that occur during a seizure. Indeed, it's hard to breathe when you burst out laughing. From a biological standpoint, it isn't too good since it causes you to hypoventilate.

But I think it's somewhat different when you're smiling. I've been feeling very comfortable watching the gentle smile on your face as you've been speaking (*laughs*), and there must be meaning to the act of smiling.

Koike: A smile is also a message of acceptance. It says you approve of the person to whom you're speaking.

Ikegaya: Yes, it has a social meaning. Besides, we're recently beginning to understand that smiling also has meaning to the person who's doing the smiling.

There's an experiment where you hold a pen in your mouth in one of two ways. The first is to place it in your mouth like a cigarette, with one end of the pen inside your mouth and the other end sticking out, and the second is to hold the pen sideways between your lips. Holding the pen in each of these two ways, you then give a score out of ten to a manga comic as you read it.

Although subjects in this experiment were reading the same comic, the average score was around 4.7 when they read the comic with the pen sticking out of their mouth. When they held the pen sideways, the average score rose to about 6.6.

The corners of your mouth are lifted when you hold a pen sideways. That seems to be the key – similar to the way in which the facial muscles move when you smile. That's different from laughing, but the experiment revealed that when you're forced to smile, you tend to enjoy more what you're doing.

Studies were recently conducted on the brain's responses when a pen is held sideways in the mouth as in the experiment. It was then discovered that what is called the reward system becomes active. Specifically, there were grounds to suggest that dopamine pathways may become active.

It shows that we're starting to find evidence that merely lifting the corners of our mouths can lighten up our mood at the neural circuit level.

Koike: You're saying that if we want to be happy, we should wear a happy smile on our face.

Ikegaya: Precisely. The paper also discusses another interesting experiment. You get a large sheet of paper and write words all over it, such as 'desk', 'cup', 'book', and so on, including positive words such as 'joy' and 'happiness', and then have your subject look for those positive words.

It takes time to find them because you've written so many words, but it's recently been discovered that subjects can find positive words more quickly than average when they hold a pen sideways in their mouth. You not only start to enjoy looking at the words; you will also improve your power of detection to find the items that make you happy. It's also interesting that you can control this physically.

Koike: I think that is indeed what we call karma in Buddhism – how attending to our actions in the present can help us in the future. For example, when you're concentrating on your work and things are going well, you won't be aware of the people sitting next to you who have started to argue. But when you're feeling down, the noise will easily enter your mind, and you will become irritated by the commotion they're causing. In other words, you aren't being irritated by the noise because it's there; you perceive the noise negatively because you're irritated.

When you're concentrating, you don't need to acknowledge information coming from the person next to you. But when you start to get frustrated, you then consciously attend to the noise they're making and allow yourself to be provoked, or maybe you take out your annoyance in some way, such as by picking up a book written by an author you dislike and reading it angrily.

Ikegaya: The external information doesn't change, yet depending on your current state, you perceive and interpret it differently. It's a matter of unconsciously setting your values for receiving information: for example, this piece of information makes you feel uncomfortable in your current state, but if you adjust your perception of it, you can just overlook it.

DOES THE BRAIN REST?

Koike: By the way, the words *Give your brain a break* are printed on the wrap-around band of my book, which the editorial staff came up with, but what about that idea of the brain taking a rest?

Ikegaya: The brain *is* continuously being used. All I can say is that the text on your wrap-around band is questionable (*laughs*). But just like the silence we've been discussing, I reckon this description of resting the brain is being used in a different way.

Koike: You can think about using your brain or letting it rest, but it isn't as if we can control it directly. What's truly important is to forget about your brain and think about allowing the unnecessary thoughts in your mind to rest – as in *Recommendation for giving your thoughts a rest*, though I'm not sure how catchy that would sound (*laughs*).

Ikegaya: There's something called the DMN, or default mode network, a network of interacting regions of the brain that becomes active when we're resting.

When studying the brain, we usually measure the level of activity in the brain when a subject is doing something, such as when they look at something in a particular colour or use their right hand, for example. But one researcher investigated what happens to the level of activity within the brain when we're just sitting absently without doing anything. That's how this DMN circuit was discovered.

Although it had initially been seen as a one-off experiment, it's now had a big take-up among neuroscientists. Some people even say that it may represent the level of activity within the brain during introspection, though we don't know that for sure yet.

This default state also exists in monkeys. Monkeys were found to have an activated DMN identical to that in humans. In any event, we have come to understand that the DMN is active when the brain is resting. It's very intriguing and indicates that neural activity during this state is consistent and very orderly.

Some papers say studies of DMN activity may be beneficial for the preliminary diagnosis of Alzheimer's disease. It all comes down to what precisely this default state is.

Koike: I think I can understand how this DMN would be used for the preliminary diagnosis of Alzheimer's. When we enter a state of deep concentration during meditation, our awareness is crystal clear, yet we see things akin to dreams, and we're also very relaxed. And when we become consciously aware of those dream-like things, our mind's movements become orderly.

I hypothesize that similar things happen when we dream while we sleep, and information that causes us discomfort becomes fragmented as if we've put it through a shredder. Then we put the pieces back together and sort through them, and by doing that, I think we're trying to reduce our discomfort or stress level.

I have a sense that with the activation of the DMN where the brain rests, we're repairing the psychological damage within us by freeing our mind from noise and making it clear, and also repairing any physical damage in the process.

Ikegaya: Maybe it's a period for recovery in mind and body.

CONCENTRATION IS NOT AN OBJECTIVE; IT'S ONLY A TOOL

Ikegaya: My belief is that science has things in common with philosophy. Listening to you talk about Buddhism, there are concrete definitions, and I do not hear about interpretations that are sentimental. In that sense, I think Buddhism is very scientific.

Koike: I don't meditate in the standard Japanese Buddhist way, but rather in the primitive or pre-sectarian Buddhist style. Zen meditation in Japan has been combined with and is greatly influenced by Chinese Taoism in practical terms. Primitive Zen meditation before that had been very systematic and scientific in its approach.

Ikegaya: I've seen data on the brain waves of Tibetan monks while they meditate. Is their method of meditation different from what you practise?

Koike: Tibetan Buddhists often engage in focused meditation, and some of their methods are similar to the one I practise.

Ikegaya: The brain waves of Tibetan monks as they meditate are completely unique. They release powerful gamma waves. We've learned that the longer a monk has trained, the more gamma waves he releases.

But Tibet does not currently allow entry to brain researchers. It's because our studies of their brain waves would give away whether the monks meditate well or poorly. Measurements of a very high-ranking monk's brain waves were once taken, revealing that he wasn't meditating at all (*laughs*). That hadn't been the case with his disciples. Their brain waves were found to be releasing gamma rays. That wasn't a very good outcome for them, and they stopped cooperating with us altogether.

Koike: That's funny (*laughs*).

Ikegaya: Gamma waves are brain waves that tend to occur when you're concentrating on something and stop to ask yourself, '*What's this?*'

When you think about it, concentration is a peculiar thing. People generally say it's good to concentrate, but it means you aren't paying attention to other things, which we have to admit is strange from a biological standpoint. For example, a wild animal shouldn't focus only on one thing. It needs to pay attention to all sorts of things that go on around it; otherwise it wouldn't notice a predator that might be approaching. Concentration is therefore potentially a threat to our lives.

But people can produce good results when they concentrate on their work or their studies. Meditation is also concentration on a single point, and I think we humans are strange beings in our ability to create these types of unnatural conditions artificially.

Koike: You're talking about our ability to shut out information in the outside world. It feels very comfortable to focus only on a single point.

Ikegaya: Yes, and I wanted to ask you about that. You become comfortable because you're shutting out everything else. It's good for the individual since they're feeling relaxed, but is a sense of comfort good for them as a living organism?

Koike: You concentrate on that sense of comfort and then erase it from your awareness. Then you can shut out the awareness of that highly relaxed state without being attached to it. When a person can erase even a tremendous state of happiness generated through meditation, they will nurture a steady mind that isn't affected by the small comforts and discomforts in their daily lives. As a result, they will have better control over various emotions.

Ikegaya: I think that's great, but we can also consider this from a negative perspective and interpret meditation as an escape from reality, can't we?

Koike: When we ask ourselves why we meditate, it comes down to seeing meditation not as a purpose, an end in itself, but rather as a tool. Once we achieve a substantial level of concentration, we start to see the flow of our awareness. We're shocked to discover what we've really been thinking behind the noise and superficial types of information. Then our mind starts to reconstruct itself, and for that, we need to have the ability to concentrate. As we decrease our attachment to pleasure and pain in this way, we stop responding reflexively and achieve a steady presence of mind that will not waver.

There was actually a time when meditation served a purpose and was not simply considered a tool. When yoga in its original form was practised, Buddha, who had been in training, learned it from a master. He arrived at the ultimate place of peace during focused meditation and was told by his master that he had reached his goal. But once he came out of meditation, Buddha became irritated and confused. He said it was not the goal and devised a self-observation method. Concentration is needed for observing oneself and reconstructing the mind. That's the purpose of meditation.

Ikegaya: So, concentration is nothing more than an interim state.

Koike: You have to be very careful, as it's true that there are people who become addicted to that state and develop a habit of escaping reality.

Ikegaya: That's very convincing. When I'm tired and want to escape reality, Zen training is one of the things that come to mind (*laughs*). Is that the wrong idea to have?

Koike: It isn't exactly the wrong mindset, but instead of providing an escape, Zen training will lead the person to face their reality more directly. In Buddhism, we have threefold training in what are known as higher virtue, a higher mind and higher wisdom. Higher virtue refers to self-imposed rules set by Buddhists. The second one, a higher mind, means to determine and to focus. It's a state in which we stop and concentrate on a single object. The last one, higher wisdom, is to observe our mind within that focused state and become aware of the patterns within us. When we do that, those patterns start to collapse, and within this flow we let go of the negative emotions within ourselves, which is the essence of our training.

This meditation method doesn't require anything physically challenging, but it's like a programme for remodelling our personality. There will be a shock, followed by changes when we take a hard look at our mind (*laughs*).

Ikegaya: I see. I wondered what it would mean from a social standpoint if people meditated and lost their fighting spirit and what would happen with our economic activities, but I can see that it's good for self-control.

Koike: Yes, whether a person is eaten up by jealousy or worried about what would happen if things don't go well at work, all concerns will disappear when they become aware that it's all about being controlled by the flow of their unconscious mind. I believe that for people today who experience stress because they're at the mercy of their mind's flow, our Buddhist methods of discipline are a very practical way to help them survive in real life.

Ikegaya: I've made a lot of discoveries today, and I'm very happy about that (*laughs*).

Koike: I very much appreciate having had the chance to hear you speak about various intriguing topics. Thank you very much.

Quick-reference chart

How to control your body and your mind

In Buddhism, we become aware of information that enters through what we call our 'six doors' – the eyes, ears, nose, tongue, body (sense of touch) and awareness. We begin to use our ability to see, hear, smell, taste, touch, think and recognize stimulation. That is how we analyse our mind.

In this book, we have been practising fundamental activities linked to the senses, such as speaking, listening and seeing. Your practice will be most effective if you know which of the six doors you may use in any given situation. In the chart here, the activities listed correspond with the numbered sections in chapter two, with those in italics matching the activities included at the end of each of the numbered sections in that chapter.

	Activity	Eyes	Ears	Nose	Tongue	Body (sense of touch)	Awareness
1	Speaking *Breathing*	Yes	Yes			Yes Yes	Yes
2	Listening *Smelling*	Yes	Yes	Yes			
3	Seeing *Laughing*	Yes Yes				Yes	
4	Reading and writing *Planning*	Yes					Yes Yes

	Activity	Eyes	Ears	Nose	Tongue	Body (sense of touch)	Awareness
5	Eating				Yes	Yes	
	Cooking					Yes	
6	Discarding	Yes					
	Buying						Yes
7	Touching					Yes	
	Waiting	Yes	Yes			Yes	
	Resting, playing and escaping					Yes Yes	
8	Nurturing						Yes
	Sleeping					Yes	

Afterword

Wishing you clean, clear thoughts

Now for the afterword for this edition. What to write? Should I write about this, or should I write about that? I can rack my brain all day, but appealing ideas do not easily come to mind.

At times like this, I always meditate to stop thinking altogether and bring my awareness back to my physical senses. It has been the same today. I stepped away from my desk for about an hour and aligned my awareness with my breathing as I sat in the morning sun, quietly watching the thoughts appear in my mind and then fade away.

As I did that, the thoughts gradually lost their strength, and a clean, clear surface began to appear in my mind as if I had scooped away the layer of foam at the top of a pan of soup cooking on the stove. Once my mind had cleared, concerns about the need to hurry up and get this finished on time for my deadline and the need to write something inspirational melted away, dispersing like the clouds in the sky.

A state like this, when the urge to write settles down, is best for writing. The mind will tense and become tense and uncooperative if dominated by thoughts of having to do something quickly or well, making it impossible to perform to one's full potential.

Readers may say, *'Okay, so it's good that your mind is clean and clear. But wouldn't the ideas stop coming if you stop thinking?'* Quite the opposite.

When you stop your thoughts for a moment, reload the information and start over with a clear mind, the distractions that interrupt information processing will quieten down. In more technical terms, we could say it's an optimization of the brain's capacity to process information.

On the other hand, reloading the information – or command, or message – that I must write an afterword for my book while my brain is full of distractions will allow my mind to do as it will and select a lot of information that's irrelevant.

An association of thoughts that follow the command *to hurry* might make me recall past jobs where I have had a tight deadline, and where I struggled to meet it. Or my subconscious mind might recreate the time that I was almost late in delivering and feeling harried as a result, bringing back memories of the pressure I was under at the time. That could very well impact upon what I'm trying to do now.

The mind often begins associating thoughts in response to a desire to do something well. Even when it isn't needed, our mind will select information from our memory to make us look good, and, as a result, we can end up with extra thoughts wafting about in our head that have nothing to do with the information that we wish to convey. That's just adding irrelevant details, and it won't be as effective in communicating our true thoughts. Our mind goes ahead and selects what it considers the most relevant pieces of information, the ones that seem to best fit at that particular time what we want to say, smoothly choosing and combining details while leaving no room for new associations of ideas to be generated. It's the klesha of desire that quietly proceeds in doing that. And naturally, the information source is limited to what we have accumulated in our memory.

When our mind stops picking unnecessary details from our memory, the result is very different. Even if the information stored in our memory is unchanged from the time our mind takes over, the results will vary, depending on our state of mind. When it's cluttered with thoughts, it will cling to similar thoughts – from our memory – and prevent us from coming up with brilliant ideas.

When our mind settles down *without thinking*, it is freed from the preconceptions or thoughts that we have up until recently. That's when things that may not seem to be connected can sometimes be drawn out of the massive amount of information preserved in our memory. It's when a new or different type of connection like that is incurred that we have inspirations.

I think we can say that fresh new ideas are not entirely new. They're born from new links in our memory, which is full of information that is not new but old, when we distance ourselves from our usual thought patterns.

That explains what has been happening since ancient times when thinkers of all kinds – whether scientists, philosophers, inventors or writers – hit a brick wall, then do something different for a change of pace and come up with an inspirational idea that leads to a breakthrough. I think it's because minds cluttered from too much thinking are calmed by the sensations associated with physical activity, such as walking or taking a bath, making it easy for them to then connect various types of information.

It isn't limited to the rarefied thoughts of scientists, inventors and writers. Maybe you're a student who can't concentrate on their studies, an entrepreneur who's waiting for a fantastic new idea, or a speaker thinking about how to fine-tune an upcoming speech. Or perhaps you're simply contemplating a new recipe or wondering where to go on your next holiday. These are beneficial principles that apply to anyone.

The world we live in is like an arena on the receiving end of carpet bombings of information and too many thoughts to process. As a result of the unexpectedly high sales of the Japanese edition of *The Practice of Not Thinking*, I have been interviewed on many occasions and asked the same question: *'Why are people buying the book?'*

I think it's because information in digital form is overwhelming us and forcing us to continue to process it in our head. We're taking in textual data from the internet on portable devices twenty-four-seven and filling our mind with that information, which is pretty stressful. Perhaps my suggestions for *practising not thinking by clearing the five senses* appeals to readers because their heads are swamped with information.

A reader once contacted me, saying that he struggled to put the book's ideas into practice and became frustrated with himself despite trying to do as the book said.

Okay. Blindly accepting what the book says as a set of golden rules can make you etch them in your mind as a sort of law that *you must act* on without thinking it through. People who are inclined to take things too literally may feel frustrated that they can't obey the rules one hundred per cent of the time. Then they'll want to give up.

A perfectionist attitude that you absolutely must stop thinking will restrict you, and that isn't how I want you to read this book. So, yes, there will be times when you *think too much*. I suggest trying *not to think* with a more relaxed attitude. Just be aware of those thoughts that come to mind and their mechanisms, and by doing so, aim to free yourself from being under their control. *The Practice of Not Thinking* is to *practise not being bound* by your thoughts.

I'm just like everyone else. There are times when the power of my meditation weakens, and various thoughts invade my mind. One example has been writing this afterword. I was stumped at the outset and couldn't get around to writing straight away. The important thing is to be aware that our thoughts are controlling our mind and to switch to *practising not being bound by our thoughts* rather than restraining ourselves or judging ourselves harshly.

The trick is to be patient, to accept that we're only human. We can activate the kind, forgiving side of our mind to avoid triggering the irritable perfectionist in us who will be frustrated when we can't do something right. When we observe our thoughts with a gentle and flexible mind, the perfectionist will calm down like a baby being stroked with a loving hand. And once settled, our thoughts will regain their energy and become crystal clear.

Thinking back, I was a past master at not being able to calm my thoughts. I studied western philosophy at university and would often play around with complex ideas in my mind and be under the illusion that I had become a refined intellectual.

I was drunk with a sense of superiority as my mind continued to come up with reasoning to interpret or criticize from a philosophical standpoint the actions of other people and society in general. My mind would be crowded with words and thoughts, with no room to relax. Thinking too much in that way will affect a person's physical well-being, and when I look back now, I can recall how I was plagued with headaches and shoulder pain during my student days. It must be because I have had plenty of first-hand experience of the harmful effects caused by a mind that processes too much linguistic information that I eventually reached the other extreme – feeling and not thinking.

I have written this book hoping that readers will maintain a clear mind, embrace the inspirations that they have, and refrain from being swallowed up by the barrage of information that hits us daily.

I will now put down my pen, praying that this edition will find new readers and the refreshing sensations of *not thinking* will spread among a wider audience.

Ryunosuke Koike

ALLEN LANE
an imprint of
PENGUIN BOOKS

Also Published

Robin DiAngelo, *Nice Racism: How Progressive White People Perpetuate Racial Harm*

Rosemary Hill, *Time's Witness: History in the Age of Romanticism*

Lawrence Wright, *The Plague Year: America in the Time of Covid*

Adrian Wooldridge, *The Aristocracy of Talent: How Meritocracy Made the Modern World*

Julian Hoppit, *The Dreadful Monster and its Poor Relations: Taxing, Spending and the United Kingdom, 1707-2021*

Jordan Ellenberg, *Shape: The Hidden Geometry of Absolutely Everything*

Duncan Campbell-Smith, *Crossing Continents: A History of Standard Chartered Bank*

Jemma Wadham, *Ice Rivers*

Niall Ferguson, *Doom: The Politics of Catastrophe*

Michael Lewis, *The Premonition: A Pandemic Story*

Richard J. Evans, *The Hitler Conspiracies: The Third Reich and the Paranoid Imagination*

Fernando Cervantes, *Conquistadores*

John Darwin, *Unlocking the World: Port Cities and Globalization in the Age of Steam, 1830-1930*

Michael Strevens, *The Knowledge Machine: How an Unreasonable Idea Created Modern Science*

Owen Jones, *This Land: The Story of a Movement*

Seb Falk, *The Light Ages: A Medieval Journey of Discovery*

Daniel Yergin, *The New Map: Energy, Climate, and the Clash of Nations*

Michael J. Sandel, *The Tyranny of Merit: What's Become of the Common Good?*

Joseph Henrich, *The Weirdest People in the World: How the West Became Psychologically Peculiar and Particularly Prosperous*

Leonard Mlodinow, *Stephen Hawking: A Memoir of Friendship and Physics*

David Goodhart, *Head Hand Heart: The Struggle for Dignity and Status in the 21st Century*

Claudia Rankine, *Just Us: An American Conversation*

James Rebanks, *English Pastoral: An Inheritance*

Robin Lane Fox, *The Invention of Medicine: From Homer to Hippocrates*

Daniel Lieberman, *Exercised: The Science of Physical Activity, Rest and Health*

Sudhir Hazareesingh, *Black Spartacus: The Epic Life of Touissaint Louverture*

Judith Herrin, *Ravenna: Capital of Empire, Crucible of Europe*

Samantha Cristoforetti, *Diary of an Apprentice Astronaut*

Neil Price, *The Children of Ash and Elm: A History of the Vikings*

George Dyson, *Analogia: The Entangled Destinies of Nature, Human Beings and Machines*

Wolfram Eilenberger, *Time of the Magicians: The Invention of Modern Thought, 1919-1929*

Kate Manne, *Entitled: How Male Privilege Hurts Women*

Christopher de Hamel, *The Book in the Cathedral: The Last Relic of Thomas Becket*

Isabel Wilkerson, *Caste: The International Bestseller*

Bradley Garrett, *Bunker: Building for the End Times*

Katie Mack, *The End of Everything: (Astrophysically Speaking)*

Jonathan C. Slaght, *Owls of the Eastern Ice: The Quest to Find and Save the World's Largest Owl*

Carl T. Bergstrom and Jevin D. West, *Calling Bullshit: The Art of Scepticism in a Data-Driven World*

Paul Collier and John Kay, *Greed Is Dead: Politics After Individualism*

Anne Applebaum, *Twilight of Democracy: The Failure of Politics and the Parting of Friends*

Sarah Stewart Johnson, *The Sirens of Mars: Searching for Life on Another World*

Martyn Rady, *The Habsburgs: The Rise and Fall of a World Power*

John Gooch, *Mussolini's War: Fascist Italy from Triumph to Collapse, 1935-1943*

Roger Scruton, *Wagner's Parsifal: The Music of Redemption*

Roberto Calasso, *The Celestial Hunter*

Benjamin R. Teitelbaum, *War for Eternity: The Return of Traditionalism and the Rise of the Populist Right*

Laurence C. Smith, *Rivers of Power: How a Natural Force Raised Kingdoms, Destroyed Civilizations, and Shapes Our World*

Sharon Moalem, *The Better Half: On the Genetic Superiority of Women*

Augustine Sedgwick, *Coffeeland: A History*

Daniel Todman, *Britain's War: A New World, 1942-1947*

Anatol Lieven, *Climate Change and the Nation State: The Realist Case*

Blake Gopnik, *Warhol: A Life as Art*

Malena and Beata Ernman, Svante and Greta Thunberg, *Our House is on Fire: Scenes of a Family and a Planet in Crisis*

Paolo Zellini, *The Mathematics of the Gods and the Algorithms of Men: A Cultural History*

Bari Weiss, *How to Fight Anti-Semitism*

Lucy Jones, *Losing Eden: Why Our Minds Need the Wild*

Brian Greene, *Until the End of Time: Mind, Matter, and Our Search for Meaning in an Evolving Universe*

Anastasia Nesvetailova and Ronen Palan, *Sabotage: The Business of Finance*

Albert Costa, *The Bilingual Brain: And What It Tells Us about the Science of Language*

Stanislas Dehaene, *How We Learn: The New Science of Education and the Brain*